# Kings and Gods of Egypt

BY

SUB-DIRECTOR OF THE MUSÉE GUIMET
PROFESSOR OF EGYPTOLOGY IN L'ÉCOLE DES HAUTES ÉTUDES (PARIS)
AUTHOR OF " IN THE TIME OF THE PHARAOHS," ETC.

TRANSLATED BY

## MADAME MORET

*WITH 36 ILLUSTRATIONS AND A MAP*

ISBN: 978-1-63923-683-1

Printed: February 2023

Published and Distributed By:
Lushena Books
607 Country Club Drive, Unit E
Bensenville, IL 60106
www.lushenabks.com

ISBN: 978-1-63923-683-1

Hatshopsitu.
(Davis, *The Tomb of Hatshopsitu*, p. 22).
Plate I.

# PREFACE

THE favourable reception given to my previous volume, *In the Time of the Pharaohs*, has encouraged me to continue my task of presenting the subject of Egyptology in popular form. The present essays were originally delivered as lectures before a cultured audience in the Musée Guimet, or written for the readers of the *Revue de Paris*.

Although as yet the results of the scholars' labours in Eastern fields have not become part of the general knowledge of the educated classes, or even of the schools and of the historians, there is in the public mind a growing interest in the discoveries made in Eastern history and art, and also an increasing demand for first-hand information presented, in non-technical language, by the specialists themselves. I have tried to meet the requirements of the thoughtful reader as well as the need of the busy student who has insufficient time to extend his reading and to gather for himself the scattered facts necessary to bring his knowledge up to date. After selecting subjects of interest I have considered these, in monographs, as exhaustively as the state of our present knowledge permits, though in a form more easily to be assimilated than the formal scholarly dissertation. While summing up the fixed points, I have pointed out certain questions that still remain unsettled, and in numerous footnotes and references I have directed the attention of the reader to the sources of information and to the discussions and comparisons of various investigations, thus securing for him a glimpse into the laboratory of research work.

My warmest thanks are extended to my wife, who has prepared the translation, and also to our common friend, Mrs. Alfred Graveson, for her kind assistance in the work of the translator. It gives me great pleasure also to acknowledge my indebtedness to my publishers of the English version, whose careful attention to all details of typography and of illustration has resulted in securing for the volume an attractive and artistic appearance.

A. M.

Paris, February, 1912.

# CONTENTS

# Contents

# PLATES

# ILLUSTRATIONS IN THE TEXT

ix

KINGS AND GODS OF EGYPT

# Kings and Gods of Egypt

## CHAPTER I

### THE QUEEN HATSHOPSITU AND HER TEMPLE OF DEIR-EL-BAHAR

DEIR-EL-BAHARI, "the Convent of the North!" The Arab name conjures up only the vision of a Coptic monastery, built by Christian congregations on the north-west confines of Thebes of the Hundred Gates—in the very heart of what is for the archæologists one of the grandest sites in the world. But the excavations of Mariette, and more especially those made under the supervision of M. Naville from 1894–1905,[1] have caused all trace of these Coptic ruins to vanish. The gaze of the visitor no longer wanders over a picturesque but squalid jumble of towers, vaults, and cells, whose

---

[1] Ed. Naville, *Deir-el-Bahari*, vol. 7 of *The Egyptian Exploration Fund*, 1894–1908; Davis and Naville, *The Tomb of Hatshopsitu*, 1906.

walls of mud and brick are crumbling in decay. To-day, beneath a glittering and luminous sky, there stand revealed a series of vast terraces and the broken ranks of white colonnades—all that remain to us of a temple of the XVIIIth dynasty, called by the Egyptians ᗱ ᗱ ⁓ *Zeser Zeserou,* "the Sublime of the Sublime."

It is one of the most interesting temples of ancient Egypt, and that, primarily, by reason of its antiquity. If we except the eastern chapels of the Pyramids of the Ancient Empire, and the Temple of the Sun, built by King Ousirniri at Abousir, of which monuments practically only the substructures remain, it is at Deir-el-Bahari that, thus far, have been found the oldest Egyptian temples; the Sublime, built about 1500 B.C., by Queen Hatshopsitu, and another sanctuary, older still by six hundred years, discovered in 1907, by M. Naville on the left side of the Sublime, for which it may have served as a model. The older structure, dating back to King Mentouhetep II, has, however, been so defaced by the ravages of time and the injuries of man that it will not bear comparison with the later temple of Queen Hatshopsitu.

This temple has a length of 750 feet and is built

against a cliff of the Libyan range, which at this point assumes the form of a semicircle, of which the northern and western arcs are honeycombed with hypogea—chambers sunk deep into the earth. The rocky ground at the foot of the cliff slopes gradually to the plain. The architect Senmout, who designed this monument, might have levelled and raised this slope into an artificial platform whereon to rear the form of temple traditional in Egypt, with pylons, colonnaded courts, hypostyle halls, and a sanctuary, such as are to be seen elsewhere in this region—in Gournah, Medinet-Habou, and the Ramesseum. But Senmout preferred to avail himself of the successive elevations of the sloping site, and therefore produced an edifice of an entirely original order, and one which was unique in Egypt (Plate II, 1). Its characteristic feature is a broad central incline which rises in a gentle grade from the plain to the Libyan hill. The idea is borrowed from the funeral chapels of the Ancient Empire. A lane of sphinxes, of which but a few remain, leads the visitor to the gate of the outer wall. Beyond the pylon, he finds himself in a vast court, stretching to right and left of the central incline. In the background behind a double row of pillars—those in the front rectangular in shape, those at the back cylindrical

—rises a stately wall of fine, white, shining limestone.  This is the first terrace and the outer
court of the temple.  Beyond it, the ground rises
fifty feet, forming a second terrace on which is
built a second court, likewise surrounded by a
white wall with a double row of pillars—all rectangular.  Here, however, the right (north) side
of the court has the additional adornment of an
unfinished colonnade, and at the end of each side
wall there rise two small temples, complete with
vestibule, hypostyle hall, and sanctuary.  That
on the left was dedicated to Hathor, that on the
right to Anubis.  The central incline leads to still
another and higher terrace, enclosed by a colonnade with a granite door, which forms the entrance
to a vestibule built against the mountain-side and
leading to the Holy of Holies, hewn in the rock
(Plate IV).  On either side of the highest terrace
a space was reserved: the one on the left, a hall of
offerings for the worship of the queen; the one on
the right, a court with an altar dedicated to the
god Râ-Harmakhis (Fig. 1).

Such, in broad outline, is the plan of this temple.
Whereas all others are characterised by a succession of halls, either covered or open, each one
forming, as it were, a screen to intercept our view
of the one beyond, here, on the contrary, we have

three successive terraces, their porticoes and colonnades showing afar off all the details of their superposed structures. There obtrude upon the eye no pylons of colossal height, no hypostyle halls with ponderous ceilings and gigantic columns;

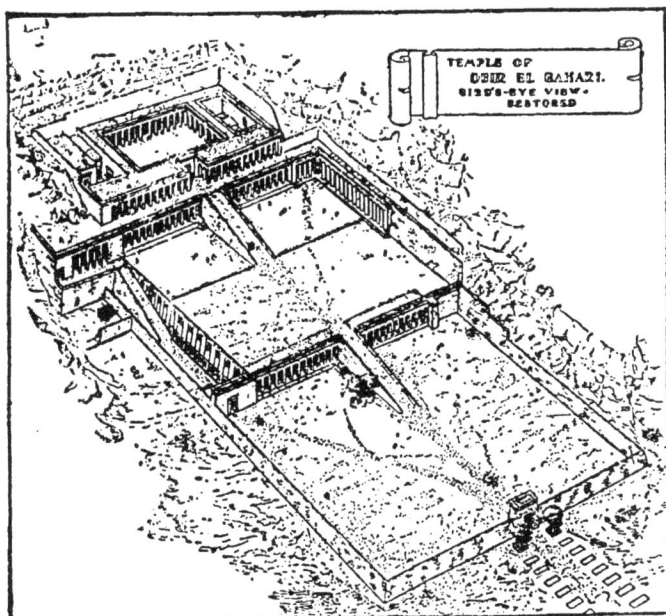

FIG. 1.—Plan of the Temple of Deir-el-Bahari, after Clarke.
(Éd. Naville, *Deir-el-Bahari*, vi, pl. 169.)

light is harmoniously distributed over the whole structure; and there are more open spaces than in other temples. All the parts, being terraced, are visible at a glance. Moreover, as the development of the colonnades makes for breadth rather than height, the necessity for huge blocks of stone is obviated, and the choicest material could be employed.   The visible parts are, consequently, built of limestone of finest texture and the most dazzling whiteness, from which the red and blue paintings stand out in bold relief.   The colonnades with their rectangular, hexagonal, or sixteen-sided columns are artistically suited to the positions they occupy and to their place in the general scheme of the structure.   All the dimensions are balanced and harmoniously proportioned, all the decoration is sober and restrained.   The pillars bear resemblance to Doric columns, to which, in fact, they have been compared (Plate III).   There is no trace here of that colossal and exaggerated style that often spoils the temples of the Ramesside dynasties.   It has often been stated that it was the Greeks who first understood the art of building peripteral edifices with external colonnades, whereas, on the contrary, the Egyptians were master-builders of monuments of colossal scale, with majestic pillars, ponderous capitals, and gigantic architraves.   This example of the Sublime is evidence that, previous to the Greeks the Egyptians fully appreciated the delicate and harmonious grace of the peristyle.   But it must be confessed that the architect Senmout had no disciples, and that after him Egypt furnishes

I. The Great Temple at Deir-el-Bahari.

II. The Incense Trees of Punt.
(Maspero, *Hist.*, *II*, p. 253).

Plate II.

scarcely another example of porticoes such as are found at Deir-el-Bahari (Plate V).

Another characteristic of the work of this innovator was to bring landscape-gardening within his architectural scheme, obtaining thereby effects of verdure rare in Egypt. For special reasons (which will be explained later), the Sublime was regarded as a kind of Garden of Eden for gods and kings. Therefore, its wide terraces and the length of its outer wall were planted with incense trees, brought at great expense, from the distant country of Punt. As may be imagined, nothing remains of these gardens save the stone basins pierced with drainage-holes, which were built into the ground and filled with soil to receive the transplanted incense trees. But if the verdure has perished, there remains, engraved for all time upon the bas-reliefs of the terrace, a tracery of these little trees with their short-stalked, crowded foliage (Plate II, 2). To-day the terraces are dismantled, no odorous foliage affords them grateful shade, yet our hearts beat with emotion as we gaze upon their pure and gracious outlines, standing forth sharp and clear against that Libyan cliff, which rises perpendicular for four hundred feet and dazzles with a burnished brilliancy, under a glowing sun. What glory must have enveloped it in

times of yore, this temple of Hatshopsitu, with its
"gardens of Amon" breathing forth sweet odours
upon the murmuring breeze, throbbing their notes
of green and gold into the symphony of colours,
through which flashed the piercing white of the
pillars, the deep tones of the paintings, and the re-
verberant russet of the rock, beneath a triumphant
sky of fathomless blue!

Hitherto we have been concerned solely with the
external appearance of the temple.   In the porticoes and buildings adjoining it, we find bas-
reliefs, from which we learn that it was constructed
about 1500 B.C., by a woman, Queen Hatshopsitu,
a daughter of Thotmes I of the XVIIIth dynasty,
the conqueror of the Syrian provinces.   The
period is the most glorious in the history of Egypt.
Victorious over her invaders, the Hyksos, Egypt
in her turn makes conquests outside her own
territory, carrying her sword and her civilisation
into Nubia and Asia, as far as the banks of the
Euphrates.   If only because it dates from this
brilliant epoch this temple would have interest for
us.   But it has, in addition, a greater claim upon
our attention.   Its inscriptions reveal that it
belongs to the class of funeral temples, and that it
served as a chapel to the tomb of Queen Hatshop-

situ. The tomb was discovered quite recently, by Mr. Davis, in the depths of the cliff. Although officially dedicated to Amon-Râ and his companion gods, Hathor and Anubis, the real divinity, whose glory the temple was intended to commemorate, was the Queen herself. The most elaborate pictures and longest inscriptions are, therefore, devoted to an account of the life of the Queen, to the description of her birth, coronation, and the most memorable event of her reign—an expedition to the land of Punt, whence were brought the incense trees planted on the terraces. Other monuments,—two obelisks and a sanctuary in the great temple of Karnak, also an inscription in a chapel of Stabel-Antar,—have thrown some light upon the glorious reign of Queen Hatshopsitu, but Deir-el-Bahari is in relation to her what the temples of Abydos and Gournah are to Seti I; what the Ramesseum is to Ramses I, and Medinet-Habou to Ramses III—the place selected to commemorate the life and might of the Pharaoh. But in this case the Pharaoh of Deir-el-Bahari happens to be a woman. In the long line of sovereigns who ruled Egypt for over four thousand years, other women will appear who governed independently, in their own right, but the first of whom we have knowledge is Hatshopsitu, the first queen in history. Hence, apart from its artistic interest, Deir-el-Bahari is of inestimable worth as a source of information upon one of the most curious figures of the Pharaonic civilisation.

Strange, to say, in spite of her long reign of over twenty years and the imperishable monuments that reign bequeathed to us, we search in vain for the name of Hatshopsitu upon the official tables of Egyptian kings inscribed at Abydos or Sakkarah, written on the Turin papyrus, or drawn up by Manetho. The Pharaohs seem to have expunged her name from their chronological records; the state archives ignore her, merely stating that Thotmes I, father of Hatshopsitu, was succeeded by two of his sons, Thotmes II and Thotmes III. If now, the modern historian, amazed at the silence of the royal documents, returns to the monuments in order to wrest from them the truth he fails to derive from official sources, he finds that all the inscriptions relating to Hatshopsitu's reign are hammered out; he can read them only by conjecture. In the bas-reliefs the face of the queen is always completely destroyed; her name effaced, mutilated, or, worse still, replaced by that of another sovereign, sometimes that of her father Thotmes I, sometimes that of her brothers, Thotmes II and Thotmes III.

From this, we conclude that Queen Hatshopsitu was the object of a veritable persecution. Why were her father and her brothers successively leagued against her? The presence of her father, whom she outlived, among her persecutors, indicates that the family strife began before his death, that she emerged from it triumphantly, but that her sovereignty was not acknowledged by her successors. The reign of Hatshopsitu presents itself to us as an historical enigma, the key to which is to be found in the ruins of Karnak and Deir-el-Bahari.[1] Let us try to follow the changing fortunes of her life, the phases of the obscure struggle in which she was now successful, now defeated, and, in which finally, she was entirely victorious.

The contest between the Thotmes and Queen Hatshopsitu sprang from a question of dynastic rights. According to the Egyptian belief, the Pharaohs were the authentic sons of the Sun Râ, in the direct line. To avoid the contamination of the solar blood by alliance with a stranger, it became an established custom for the sons and daughters of the kings, brothers and sisters, to

[1] Kurt Sethe, *Die Thronwirren unter den Nachfolgern Kgs. Thutmosis I*, 1896.

marry among themselves; and the children of such marriages alone were regarded as the true sons of the gods, legitimate heirs of the throne. Sometimes, however, it happened that, owing to degeneration of the race or to some other reason, the sons and daughters of the kings had to take a consort, one in whose veins did not flow the solar blood. Such a case occurred at the beginning of the XVIIIth dynasty. King Thotmes I was born from such an inferior union. His mother, Senousenb, bore the title "mother of the king," not "spouse of the king"; she seems, therefore, to have been only a concubine.[1] But Thotmes I, himself, married a legitimate princess, who had the power to confer upon her husband her regal rights. It was through these rights that Thotmes I occupied the throne on behalf of and together with his wife, Queen Ahmasi. Thotmes I and Queen Ahmasi had four children, two sons and two daughters. The two sons, Amenmes and Ouazmes,[2] died young; so the heir to the throne was the elder daughter, our future Queen Hatshopsitu. But Thotmes had also two bastard sons: one, whose mother bore the title of "royal

[1] See the rescript of the accession of Thotmes I, *Aegyptische Zeitschrift*, xxix, p. 117.

[2] Mentioned in a funeral chapel at Gournah, pub. Grébaut, *Musée Égyptien*, i, Pl. 6.

wife"[1] (that is to say, a queen of an inferior rank, never named "chief spouse of the king") became, later, Thotmes II; the other, born of a simple concubine ("Gsit, wife of the king," yet not "chief spouse of the king") is known to history as Thotmes III.[2]

That these illegitimate sons could seize the throne and gain official recognition to the detriment of the claims of the rightful heir, their sister, Queen Hatshopsitu, can, to my mind, be explained only by the existence of an opposition party at the Egyptian court. This party would not, on any terms, entrust to a woman, incapable of bearing arms or of commanding an army in the field, the destinies of Egypt, at a time when she had entered upon a career of conquest and was striving for an expansion of her dominions beyond their present limits. The result was that the question of women's rights arose and was fought out between two parties, one struggling to support the legiti-

[1] She is the "wife of the king, mother of the king," Moutnefrit, known by a statue that her son Thotmes II consecrated to her. *Aegyptische Zeitschrift*, 1887, p. 125.

[2] According to this hypothesis, Thotmes II and Thotmes III were half-brothers of Hatshopsitu (London, Statue of Anebni, where Thotmes III is called brother of the queen, *ap.* Lepsius, *Auswahl*, Pl. 11). Ed. Naville, on the contrary, following a text at Karnak and the inscription of Anna, considers Thotmes II as father of Thotmes III. *Cf. post*, p. 29.

mate claims of Hatshopsitu, the other trying to bring about her downfall.

The struggle began on the death of the Queen Ahmasi. Illegitimate by birth, king only while he was the husband of a queen, Thotmes I, was now an interloper on the throne. The legitimist party, though they owed a debt of gratitude to the great king who had achieved so much for the glory of Egypt, compelled him to abdicate and yield the power to Hatshopsitu. She married and placed upon the throne as joint ruler her half-brother Thotmes (the one we call Thotmes III), probably the elder of the two illegitimate sons of the deposed King. According to the royal tables, which we know have been falsified, it is Thotmes II who succeeded Thotmes I, and there are still a few Egyptologists who accept the statement. But if we refer to the monuments, it is quite clear that Hatshopsitu and Thotmes III were crowned on the same day[1] and reigned together prior to the Thotmes who is described on the tables as Thotmes II. Of the first two years of their joint reign, little is known, save that the queen during this period

---

[1] The "day of the enthronement" of Thotmes III and of the queen is on the 4th Pakhons; positive proof, says Sethe (§17-18) of the common accession of brother and sister. The accession of Thotmes II, whom other scholars regard as the husband of the queen, is on the contrary on the 8th of Paophi.

Cliché Doucet.

Deir-el-Bahari.    The Unfinished Portico.

Plate III.

appears in the subordinate position of a consort. Her title is the one common to all queens
⸢𓎡𓏤𓏏𓈖𓌳⸣.[1] On certain monuments, such as the
temple of Semneh,[2] the name of Thotmes III
appears alone. There is no mention of the Queen,
neither her presence nor her name. The King
acts without her.

This is not fair play and we are led to think
that the truth is not fully revealed. It seems
indeed as if Thotmes III had occupied the throne
even before the accession of the legitimate heir,
Hatshopsitu. Was this due to a conspiracy on
the part of the priests of Amon? Let us hear
what the king himself had to say upon the subject:

As a young man I was in the temple before I was
raised to the dignity of a prophet. . . . I played the
part of Anmoutef,[3] like the young Horus of Khemmis;
I stood upright in the northern part of the hypostyle.
There was held a great festival of heaven and earth,
. . . during which the god received (on) his altar
in the temple the wonderful gifts of the people (offered
by the king). . . . His Majesty placed before the
god incense on the fire and offered to him a great
oblation of oxen, calves, and mountain goats. The
god paced along two sides of the hypostyle; the heart
of those walking before him understood not what he

---

[1] Sethe, § 31, "spouse of the god; chief spouse of the king."
[2] Dated from the year 2. (Lepsius, *Denkmäler*, iii, 55a.)
[3] Priest of the royal worship.

did, while he was seeking My Majesty everywhere.
When the god recognised me he halted. . . . I prostrated myself in his presence.  He caused me to stand
in front of him, and lo!  I was put in the *Place of the
King*.  He was amazed to see me . . . and then were
revealed to the people the secrets that lay in the heart
of the god and were known to none. . . .  He opened
for me the portals of the horizon of Râ.  I soared to
heaven, like a divine falcon beholding his own shape
in the skies; I adored His Majesty. . . .  I saw the
glorious form of the god of the horizon on his mysterious paths in the heaven.[1]  Râ himself established
me (king); I was consecrated with the diadems which
were upon his head, and his uræus was placed (on my
brow) . . . I received the dignities of a king . . .
and my great royal names were given me.[2]

In spite of this divine sanction, bestowed upon
him by the priests of Amon, Thotmes III could not
make valid his claim to the throne otherwise than
by marriage with the legitimate heir, Hatshopsitu.
But she was ambitious and found partisans to
support her rights.  A plot of the priestly and
anti-feminist party was met by a counter-plot of
the legitimist party.  This came to pass between

---

[1] Amon-Râ is a solar god who dwells in the sky.  Hence the
terms *the sky, the horizon of Râ* are used as mystical designators of
the sanctuary where dwells the statue of Amon-Râ before which
the royal candidate is brought; he is then supposed to be carried
up to heaven like a falcon (Horus) soaring to the sun.

[2] From an inscription carved on the outer side of the south wall
of the sanctuary at Karnak—lately published with commentary
by Breasted, *A New Chapter in the Life of Thutmose III*, 1900.

the years 2 and 5 of the reign about the time when Hatshopsitu began to build the temple of Deir-el-Bahari. From this date onward, Hatshopsitu, who up to the present has been known only as "chief wife of the king," assumes all the designations that are the prerogative of the king. She is called "female Horus," 𓃒, "female Râ" 𓇳 ; and the full title of a king is bestowed upon her ↓ ⸗ , the double cartouche and the usual fourfold names, as can be seen in the two series of bas-reliefs relating to the birth and enthronement, that she caused to be engraved in her temple of Deir-el-Bahari.

These bas-reliefs were intended to remind her people that of the royal pair, it is she alone who, as the direct offspring of Amon-Râ, has the actual right to sit upon the throne. The theory of the solar descent can be traced back to a very remote past. The first evidence we have of its practical application dates from the years of the Vth dynasty, when the kings assumed the title of "sons of the Sun" 𓅷𓇳 ; a title, which from that time on was constantly borne by them. But to our knowledge, Hatshopsitu is the first sovereign who had the circumstances of the royal birth set forth pictorially, and with elaborate detail, on the walls of a temple. Testimony to her divine origin would help her to enforce her rights. Therefore, to convince the people of her legitimacy, she caused to be engraved upon the walls of the middle terrace of the temple a picture showing

FIG. 2.—Amon-Râ and the Queen.

the carnal union of the god Amon-Râ with her mother Ahmasi (Fig. 2).

The god and the queen are represented sitting face to face, their legs crossed, on a state bed ornamented with the head and feet of a lion. The queen receives from her husband the symbols of life and strength (⚲↑); the two goddesses, Neit and Selkit, protectors of conjugal unions, support the feet of the royal pair, and guard their persons from all evil. The lyric text, inscribed around the picture, leaves no doubt regarding the material nature of the union.

These were the words of Amon-Râ, king of the gods, lord of Karnak, he who rules at Thebes, when he took upon himself the form of that male, the king of the South and of the North, Thotmes I, giver of life. He found the queen sleeping amidst the splendours of her palace. The perfume of the god awoke her, and, when His Majesty marched straight towards her, knew her, laid his heart against hers, and made himself known unto her in his godly aspect, she marvelled greatly! And when he had revealed himself, she was enraptured by the knowledge of his beauties; her love for the god coursed through her being and the odour of the god and of his breath were fragrant with all the fragrance of Punt.

And these were the words of the spouse of the king, the mother of the king, Ahmasi, in the presence of the majesty of this august god, Amon, lord of Karnak, master of Thebes: "Twice great are thy souls! It is a *noble* thing to view thy *face* when *thou knowest* My Majesty in the fulness of thy grace! Thy dew flows through all my members!" Then, when the majesty of the god had accomplished all his desire with her, Amon, the god of the two lands, thus spoke unto her: "*She who unites herself with Amon, the first of the beloved,* behold! such shall be the name of the daughter who shall open thy womb, since those are the words that have fallen from thy lips. She shall exercise a beneficial power over all this land, for my soul is hers, my will is hers, my crown is hers, verily! that she may govern the two lands and guide all the living doubles.[1]

---

[1] *Deir-el-Bahari*, ii, Pl. XLVII, text completed by that of Luxor (*Recueil de travaux*, ix, p. 84). The Egyptians tried to remember the words that the mother uttered at the moment of conception (they are the words underlined in the text) and made from them a name of good omen for the child. *Cf.* A. Moret, *Du caractère religieux de la royauté pharaonique*, p. 50 *et seq.* (*Annales du Musée Guimet, Bibliothèque d'études*, t. xv).

On other bas-reliefs of Deir-el-Bahari are represented scenes which portray the preparations,
the *accouchement*, and the delivery of the Queen.
Khnoumou the divine potter, who gives their
forms to gods and men, declares to Amon that he
will so fashion the royal child that her beauty shall
surpass the beauty of the gods, so that she may
be the better fitted to fulfil her mission as ruler of
the two lands.[1]   The following scene shows us
Ahmasi in labour (Fig. 3).   The Queen is seated
in an arm-chair which is placed on a platform
shaped like a bed; Isis and Nephthys hold her
by the arms, according to the eastern custom;
the new-born child is presented to protecting goddesses, who breathe into her and her double the
breath of life.  Then is shown the presentation of
the child to Amon, her real father, who "clasps,
caresses, and rocks her whom he loves above all
things." and addresses to her these words of
welcome: "Come, come in peace, daughter of my
loins, whom I love, royal image, thou who wilt
make real thy risings on the throne of the Horus of
the living, for ever!"[2]   Next, Hatshopsitu is shown

The figures 2 and 3 are reproduced from the bas-reliefs of Luxor
(after Gayet, Pl. 63 and 65), those at Deir-el-Bahari being
too mutilated for reproduction.

[1] *Deir-el-Bahari*, ii, Pl. XLVIII.
[2] *Ibid.*, ii, Pl. LI–LIII.

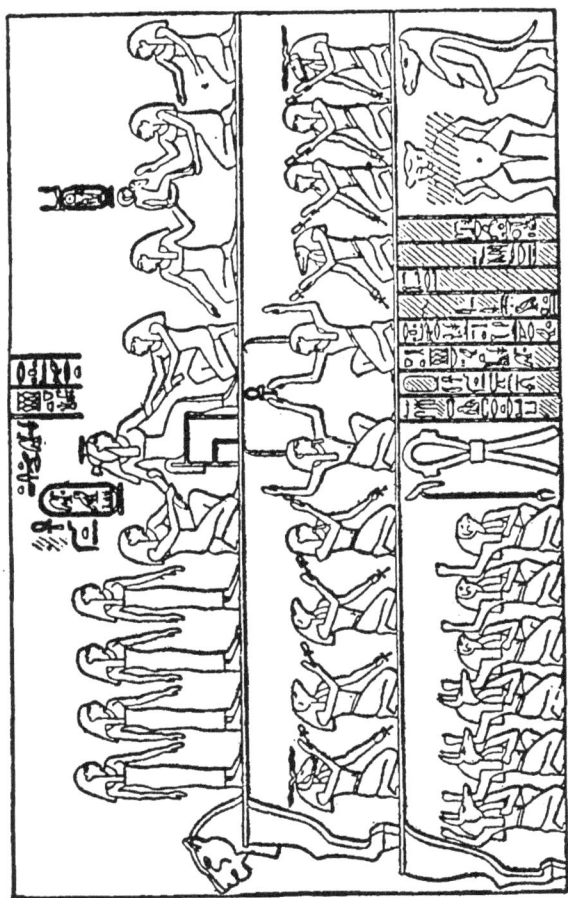

FIG. 3.—Birth of the Pharaoh.

acknowledged and worshipped by the other gods, while the divine promises made to her are duly inscribed upon the celestial books.[1]

Such bas-reliefs of the theogony and birth of Hatshopsitu were certainly injurious to the bastard Pharaoh, Thotmes III, who could not, like his queen, boast of a divine origin. Nor could he find pleasure in other pictures which formed a sequence to these and showed how Hatshopsitu, called to the throne by her divine father, Amon-Râ, was crowned indeed by her human father Thotmes I, and became Queen of Egypt through the will of the gods and of men.

As a reply to the inscription telling how Thotmes III received the crown from the hands of Râ, when the machinations of the priesthood placed him on the throne, Hatshopsitu desired to be depicted wearing the *pschent*, after a visit to the gods of Heliopolis. There, Atoum placed the diadem upon her head, as a suggestion to the Egyptians and to the gods of Thebes to establish her queen of Egypt. What her age may have been at this time we do not know. The texts tell us only that "Her Majesty was growing above all things . . . she was beautiful to look upon above all things

[1] A. Moret, *Du caractère religieux de la royauté pharaonique,* pp. 53-59.

Cliché Doucet.

Deir-el-Bahari.   Entrance to the Subterranean Sanctuaries.

Plate IV.

. . . she was like unto a god; her form was that of a god; she did everything like a god; her splendour was that of a god; Her Majesty was a maiden, fair and in her bloom. . . ."[1]

Then we hear that one day, in that spring-time of her youth, Thotmes I, seated on a high throne in the royal hall, called together his nobles, his dignitaries, his friends, the court slaves, and the state officials, that they might witness the following scene. The King, seated, placed his daughter in front of him, embraced her, and proceeded to make the magic passes of the *setep sa*[2] while the whole assembly, prostrate on the ground, aided in the sending forth of the protective magic fluid. Thotmes I then appealed to those present, to acknowledge their new ruler:

This, my living daughter, Khnoumit-Amon Hatshopsitu, I place in my seat; I set her on my throne. Behold! she sits upon my throne; she makes her words heard in all parts of the palace; verily, she guides you. Hearken to her words and submit yourselves to her commands. He who adores her, behold! he shall live. He who speaks evil against Her Majesty, behold! he

[1] *Deir-el-Bahari*, iii, Pl. LVII

[2] In order to send forth the *setep sa*, which ensures to an individual magic protection, the operator is represented standing behind him with outstretched hand raised along his neck or his back. From its analogy to hypnotic passes, we translate *setep sa* by the expression "send forth the fluid of life."

shall die. Let all those who hearken to her and with their whole hearts accept the name of Her Majesty come, even now, to proclaim her Queen beside me. Verily! this daughter of the gods is divine, and the gods fight for her and shed their fluid [of life] upon her neck every day, as was ordained by her father, the lord of the gods.

This address of the King was received with great favour by the assembly, who "proclaimed" the royal name of the new Pharaoh.

The royal nobles, the dignitaries, the chief officials listened to the announcement that she possessed the dignity of daughter of the king, that she was queen of the South and of the North, *Mait ka ri* that she would live forever. They grov- elled at her feet; they prostrated themselves at her royal command to adore all the gods adored by her father, King Thotmes I.

Then the *nekheb* or protocol of her new royal names was drawn up, and Amon-Râ so inspired the priests whose duty it was to bestow these names upon her "that they chose even those that he had given her already" at the moment of his union with Queen Ahmasi.

After this investiture by men, Hatshopsitu had still to "receive her crowns from the lords of the divine dwellings," that is, from the gods of Thebes. The first ceremony represented is a purification.

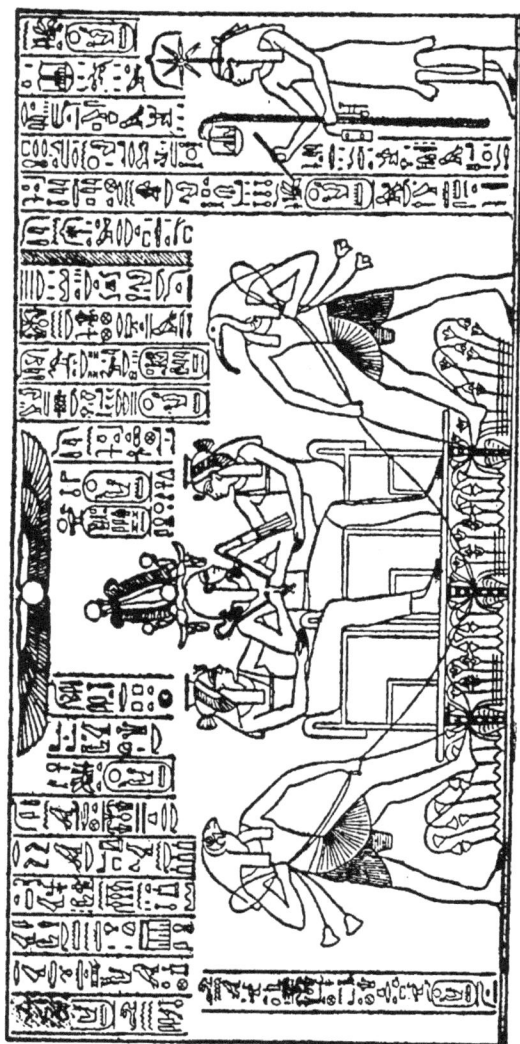

FIG. 4.—The Coronation of the Pharaoh.
(Mariette, *Abydos*, I, pl. 31 a.)

After this, Hatshopsitu enters the sanctuary, pre-
ceded by the old historical ensigns of the Egyptian
nomes.  She goes first to the naos of the South,
where the gods Horus and Seth[1] place on her head
the white crown of the South ⚑ .  She then pro-
ceeds to the naos of the North, where she receives
the red crown of the North ⚐ .  This ceremony
was called the rising of the king of the South and
the rising of the king of the North.  Next, the
Queen wearing the *pschent* ⚑, or double crown,
is seen seated on a throne between two divinities
of the South and the North.  Beneath the royal
seat were placed flowers of the lotus, the plant of
the South, and branches of papyrus, the plant of
the North.  These are tied together by cords
which are crossed around a central pillar; the gods
Horus and Seth draw the cords tight with their
hands (Fig. 4), and hold them firm with their
feet so that lotus and papyrus may be drawn
together.  This rite was called *sam taoui*.  It
symbolised the "union of the two lands of the
North and South" under the feet of the Queen.
Finally, Hatshopsitu, her crown upon her head,
a great mantle upon her shoulders, holding in her

---

[1] Represented by two priests wearing, one the head of a hawk
(Horus), the other, the head of a Typhonian animal (Seth) or the
head of an ibis (Thot).

hands the scourge and staff of Osiris, walks in procession "round the wall" of the sanctuary, in order to take possession of it and to assure the protection "of the domain of Horus and the domain of Seth." This done, the new queen is led in great pomp to Amon, her celestial father, who embraces her, and she enters definitively upon the mission, more divine than human, that devolves upon the Pharoah.[1]

Throughout this detailed account of the enthronement of Hatshopsitu by her human father, Thotmes I, and by the Theban gods, no mention is ever made of her husband, Thotmes III; no reference, even, to his existence. This leads to the supposition that the Queen had the pictures engraved after a successful attempt of her party to place her on the throne. This revolution thrust Thotmes III to one side, without depriving him of the title of king, but made the Queen the actual ruler. This story of her coronation by her father, Thotmes I, which we have just examined, is but an historical fiction, designed for the edification

[1] *Deir-el-Bahari*, iii, Pl. LX, *et seq.* All these ceremonies, as old as the Egyptian monarchy, are represented in pictures or mentioned in proto-historic records; they preserve a remembrance of the mythical kingship of Horus and Seth, who, according to tradition, reigned before the human kings. Detailed description and signification will be found in A. Moret, *Du caractère religieux de la royauté pharaonique*, pp. 79-113.

of her subjects. We have seen that after the deposition of Thotmes I, it was in reality Thotmes III, who seized the power, because he held his rights from his wife, Hatshopsitu, in the same manner as his father held his from his wife, Queen Ahmasi. But Thotmes III had neglected to have his queen represented beside him on the monuments. Now that a turn of fortune places her on the throne, Hatshopsitu treats him in like manner, and she appears alone in all representations of regal functions.

How strange and difficult, however, must have been her position is evidenced by the very texts and pictures at Deir-el-Bahari. The Egyptians seem to have offered strenuous opposition to the idea of a female Pharaoh. But though at Deir-el-Bahari, the texts speak of her in feminine terms, the pronouns referring to her being always "she" and "her," and the royal or divine titles assumed by her are transcribed in the feminine form, 𓄿, 𓂝, 𓏏𓏤, 𓏏𓏤, etc., it is obvious that she was at great pains to conceal her sex. In the pictures of her birth, the child presented to the gods is unquestionably a male. In the pictures of the coronation she is represented as wearing the traditional state dress of the kings, a short loin-cloth, a false beard, and a plaited tail hanging behind from her loins;

while her uncovered breast is distinctly masculine. She even tried to change the very name
she had received at her birth and to mascu-
linise it by omitting the feminine ending. She
modified Hatshopsitu, "the first of the beloved women," into Hatshopsiu, "the first of
the nobles" (Plate I). Do not these rather
clumsy stratagems imply a fear lest the court
and the people should distrust her, because
she was a woman and, therefore, unable to
fulfil all the duties which a man-ruler regards
as inseparable from the exercise of the kingly
office?

This brilliant period in the life of Hatshopsitu
lasted only about eighteen months. Towards the
end of the year 6, monuments, such as those of
Deir-el-Bahari, appear to us to undergo a change.
The texts concerning the birth and enthronement
are pitilessly hammered out, the figures of the
Queen are completely destroyed. In those cases
where some outline remains, a singular inter-
ference may be remarked: the names of Hatshopsitu and of Thotmes III are replaced by those of
Thotmes I, and of his second son Thotmes II;
while for the Queen's figure when she is in the
presence of a god, there is substituted the design

of an altar[1] in order to retain some signification for the picture. For example, on a certain obelisk, the Queen was represented as seated before the god Amon, bowing her neck before him in order to receive his blessing. The restorers have transformed the picture thus: The god stretches out his hand to take the offerings placed on two little altars which occupy the place of the original figure of the Queen, still visible, in spite of the hammering out of its contours. What conclusion is to be drawn from this evidence? The following, it would appear. The Queen and her husband Thotmes III were dispossessed and replaced by the very men whose names are superimposed on the former and who made these alterations,[2] Thotmes I and Thotmes II. That would explain why in the chapels of Anubis[3] and Hathor which are of later date than the bas-reliefs of the birth and enthronement, the royal donors are no longer Hatshopsitu and Thotmes III, but Thotmes I and Thotmes II, who up to this time have never appeared in this rôle in the parts of the temple built at an earlier date.

[1] Sethe, *loc cit.*, § 46.
[2] Sethe, §22–24. The conjecture that Hatshopsitu was perse-cuted by Thotmes II had already been admitted by E. de Rougé.
[3] With the wooden shrine of which we have preserved the panels (*Deir-el-Bahari* ii, 27–29).

Deir-el-Bahari.    Entrance to Anubis Chapel.

Plate V.

Was this restoration of masculine government brought about by the exigencies of military expeditions which it seemed unfitting should be led by a queen? Be that as it may, Thotmes I and Thotmes II are no sooner joint kings on the throne than they begin anew campaigns in Nubia and expeditions to the shores of the Euphrates.[1] The booty amassed during these wars permits them to build an altar and new chapels at Deir-el-Bahari. In the midst of all these events Thotmes I, dies, which fact is proved by a monument preserved at Turin, in which Thotmes II is represented as adoring his deceased father.[2] From an inscription recently discovered at Karnak,[3] we learn further that after the death of his father, Thotmes II, feeling his position insecure, took as his co-regent, not Hatshopsitu, but her discarded husband, Thotmes III. Their joint government lasted till the death of Thotmes II, which occurred about the year 9, two years and a half after his accession.

Fortune affords to Hatshopsitu the opportunity to recover her kingdom, which she held till her death. This is how a contemporary, Anna, describes the situation on the death of Thotmes II.

[1] According to the biographies of Anna and Ahmes, and a text at Assouan. *Cf.* Breasted, *Ancient Records*, ii, pp. 47-52.

[2] Lepsius, *Auswahl*, Pl. 11.

[3] Breasted, *Ancient Records*, ii, p. 235.

The king ascended to the Heavens and joined the company of the gods; his son [the expression means his successor, Thotmes III[1]] took his place as king of the Two Lands; he reigned on the throne of him who begat him.   His sister, the divine woman Hatshopsitu, adjusted the affairs of the two kingdoms according to her own mind.   Egypt, bowing the head before her cultivated the excellent seed divine, sprung from the god.   She was the cable which drew the North, the stake to which was moored the South; she was the perfect tiller-rope of the North, the mistress who issues commands, whose wise plans bring peace upon the Two Lands when she opens her mouth.[2]

This description of the later power of the Queen is entirely confirmed by the pictures in the temple of Deir-el-Bahari, the construction of which was resumed by her in the year 9.   The situation is exactly what it was before she was temporarily ousted from the throne by the coalition of Thotmes I and Thotmes II.   All the honours are for the Queen; as for Thotmes III, he very rarely appears in the decoration of the temple, and, then, always behind the Queen, or in the rôle of a subordinate.

How then can it be explained why Thotmes III recalled Hatshopsitu?   It must have been that

---

[1] The reading of Sethe, §7 and Breasted, *Ancient Records*, **ii, p.** 142.

[2] Biography of Anna; see also the inscription at **Karnak** (Breasted, *Ancient Records*, ii, pp. 142 and 235).

he was compelled to do so by the legitimist party. And now, this party, whose presence, thus far, has been a matter of conjecture, enters upon the scene. The leaders of it are known to us and we see them portrayed upon the walls of Deir-el-Bahari. They are as follows:

*Senmout*, the architect of the temple, of whom we possess two statues which were granted him by the Queen. He superintended all the construction at Deir-el-Bahari, Karnak, Luxor, etc. The Queen entrusted to him the education of her daughter Neferoura, whom he holds in his lap in the statue which is preserved at Berlin. He was, at a later date, the trustee of the princess's fortune and one of the stewards of the immense domain of Amon[1] (Plate VI, 1).

*Nehsi* was the guardian of the royal seal, chief treasurer, and an intimate friend. He shared with Senmout the command of the expedition into the land of Punt.[2]

*Thoutii* administered the royal finances, as the "head of the house of the gold and of the silver."[3]

*Hâpousenb*, high-priest of Amon, chief of the prophets of the South and of the North, and, at

---

[1] *Cf.* Breasted, *Ancient Records*, ii, p. 363.
[2] *Ibid.*, ii, p. 290.
[3] *Ibid.*, ii, p. 369.

the same time, prime minister, held in his hands all civil and priestly power.[1]

Such were the leaders of the camarilla who brought about Hatshopsitu's triumph. They all took a leading part in the memorable events which followed the restoration in the year 9. The temple of Deir-el-Bahari has preserved for us a description of one of these enterprises which appears to have impressed contemporaries, namely a maritime expedition to the land of Punt.

Punt was an almost unknown region which stretched along the two shores of the Red Sea.[2] It may perhaps be placed in about the locality of Souakim and Massaouah. The Egyptians said that perfumes, incense, myrrh, precious woods, gold, and all the riches of the earth could be found in abundance in this earthly paradise, the country of the gods Horus and Hathor, the "land divine." Punt was to them a half-real, half-fabulous region of which they thought as the vague birthplace of the race, both gods and men. During the Ancient Empire and at the time of the first Theban kings,[3] several expeditions had gone thither to bring back gold, spices, and perfumes. It was to

[1] Breasted, *Ancient Records*, ii, p. 388.
[2] Mariette, *Deir-el-Bahari*, Pl. 5.
[3] Breasted, *Ancient Records*, ii, p. 102.

pay a debt of gratitude to the gods Amon and Hathor, whose priests had finally supported her rights, that as soon as Hatshopsitu was established once more on the throne, she sent her most faithful agents, Senmout, Nehsi, and Thoutii on an embassy to Punt (Fig. 5).[1]

FIG. 5.—A Village in the Land of Punt.

In fact, the gods had expressed their will in the matter. One day, "the prayers of the sovereign rose to the throne of the lord of Karnak and a command was heard in the sanctuary, an oracle from the god himself, that the ways to Punt should be explored, and the roads searched out which lead to the land of the Incense." "I have given

[1] Davis and Naville, *The Tomb of Hatshopsitu*, p. 32.

thee Punt," says the god elsewhere, "none knew
the way to the country of the gods, none had gone
up to the terraces of the Incense, none among the
Egyptians; but they had heard of them from the
lips of those who lived in olden times."

The fleet, composed of five ships, was heartily

FIG. 6.—Parihu, Lord of the Land of Punt,
and his Wife, Ati.

welcomed by Parihu, lord of the land of Punt,
and his wife Ati[1] (Fig. 6).   The Egyptians offered
gifts of "bread, beer, wine, meat, vegetables,—
all the things of Egypt."   In exchange, Senmout
loaded his boats with thirty-one incense trees,

[1] Notice that Parihu carries a boomerang in his hand, wears a
necklace around his neck, has a dagger thrust into his belt, and his
right leg is covered with metal rings (from their yellow colour,
possibly of gold).   His wife, and his daughter (portrayed elsewhere) are of the large and adipose type of beauty, characteristic
of the Hottentot Venus.

and "heaps of aromatic gums, ebony, ivories, gold, precious woods, incense, antimony powder, monkeys, greyhounds, besides skins of the leopards of the South, and people of the land and their children." When the expedition returned to Thebes, the incense trees were transplanted in the court of the temple, which became "the garden of Amon." All the treasures from the land of Punt were presented to the gods.

The Queen gave a silver-gilt bushel-measure to measure the heaps of gum, the first time they enjoyed the happiness of measuring the perfumes for Amon and of presenting to him the wonderful gifts that Punt produces. Thot recorded the amounts in writing. . . . Her Majesty herself prepared with her own hands an essence to perfume her limbs. She exhaled the odour of the divine dew, her fragrance reached as far as Punt, her skin was like kneaded gold, and her face shone like stars in a festal hall, before the whole earth.[1]

The fétes which followed the expedition into Punt mark, as it were, the apotheosis of the Queen and constituted the glory of the temple of Deir-el-Bahari. During the remaining years of her life (we count them as far as the year 20),[2] the Queen

___

[1] Translation of Maspero. Cf. *Histoire*, ii, p. 245 *et seq.* and *Études de mythologie et archéologie*, iv, p. 93 *et seq.*

[2] According to an expedition to Sinai, dated from the year 20 of the joint reign (Petrie, *Sinaï*, p. 19).

continued the decoration of the temple, but the building was never completed. She allowed the bas-reliefs of the first years of her reign to remain mutilated as they had been by Thotmes I and II. She did not restore them nor did she persecute the memory of either her father or her brother by hammering out their names and portraits. She seems to have spent her last years in peace and glory. Her faithful servant, Hâpousenb, undertook to hew her a tomb in the "valley of the kings," which is situated beyond the cliff that overhangs the temple. This hypogeum, which is dug out slantwise, goes very far down and the chamber is 900 feet away from the entrance. It was cleared out by Mr. Davis in 1904 who found in it two beautiful empty sarcophagi and the canopic box of Thotmes I and of the Queen his daughter.[1] The mummy of the King had some time before been found in the "well of Deir-el-Bahari." Is Hatshopsitu's, perhaps, one of the two female mummies lacking inscriptions, that have not yet been identified? So far, there has been no reply to this problem; Egypt hides from us the mortal remains of Hatshopsitu.

Is it possible that the body was sacrificed to the spite and vengeance of her enemies? Thotmes III,

[1] Davis and Naville, *The Tomb of Hatshopsitu*.

from the year 9, had occupied a subordinate, humiliating position; in the bas-reliefs of the expedition to Punt, which exalt so high the glory of his sister-queen, he is mentioned and represented only once, offering the incense he did not conquer to the gods of the Queen. But after the Queen's death, he and his party take their revenge. The temple of Deir-el-Bahari suffers again from the rage of the iconoclasts; all the inscriptions and bas-reliefs in which the Queen appears are defaced by the hammer; only the scenes which depict the land of Punt are spared—those, at least, in which she is supposed to have had no part. Even the tombs of those who had so faithfully served the Queen—Senmout, Nehsi, Thoutii, Hâpousenb— were completely sacked. Then, Thotmes III, free at last to exercise his own personal energy, to act upon his own initiative set out, in the year 22, upon the famous expeditions into Syria, which made him the greatest Egyptian conqueror.

Such are the tragic events of the story which we can reconstitute from the defaced walls of Deir-el-Bahari. It is not easy to extricate the truth in history from official falsehood, involuntary errors, and personal interpretations. The temple of Deir-el-Bahari is like a palimpsest in which we laboriously decipher the old script beneath the newer writing above it. The patient efforts of many scholars have been required to rescue from oblivion that Queen, cast out from the royal lists.[1] History presents similar enigmatic figures; among them, in France, Louis XVII, who, unlike Hatshopsitu, is counted in the chronological tables, though he never reigned.

Can it be said that Hatshopsitu was a great queen? We may suppose so. She appears to have been endowed with energy and patience, with a shrewd and subtle mind, and one recognises in her the far-away ancestress of that line of clever rulers, of whom Catherine of Russia, Elizabeth of England, and Maria Theresa of Austria are notable instances, who were able, in spite of opposition, to maintain themselves on the throne using pardon more than chastisement. She seems to have had all the qualities of a Pharaoh, and probably the only reproach that was brought against her is that she was a woman. If that caused the erasure of her name from the royal records, we will repair the prejudice of the Egyptians, by admiring at Deir-el-Bahari all that is left to us of the first woman who reigned in her own right.

---

[1] Ed. Naville does not admit the events as stated by Sethe in the royal career of Hatshopsitu. *Cf.* Davis and Naville, *The Tomb of Hatshopsitu.*

# CHAPTER II

## THE RELIGIOUS REVOLUTION OF AMENOPHIS IV

IN spite of the fact that many of his monuments have been preserved for us, Amenophis IV,[1] who reigned about 1370 B.C., is of all the Pharaohs the most curious and at the same time the most enigmatic figure. In this land of Egypt, where tradition is all-powerful, amongst a people, "the most religious of all men,"[2] who had remained faithful to their gods for thousands of years, Amenophis IV devised and carried out a religious revolution, the disestablishment and disendowment of the great national god, Amon-Râ. He substituted for Amon the god Aton, whose worship he imposed upon the court, the priests, the Egyptian people, and foreign subjects.

To sever the relations between the state and the sacerdotal class, who administer the official religion, has proved an arduous task in any country

[1] Amenophis is the Greek transcription of the Egyptian name Amonhetep or Amenhotep.
[2] Expression used by Herodotus.

and in any age; but what particular difficulties did such a revolution mean in Egypt? Amenophis IV, like all the Pharaohs, his ancestors—we have already had an instance in Hatshopsitu—was regarded as the son and heir of the gods, and in particular as the successor of Amon-Râ, the patron god of Thebes, which had become the capital of Egypt under the New Empire. Upon the temple walls were sculptured the scenes which testified to the begetting of the King by the god.[1] At Luxor, for example, was represented the carnal union of Amon with the Queen Moutemouâ, mother of Amenophis III, the father of our revolutionary king. Another picture showed the Queen being delivered, with the help of the goddesses, and bringing forth a child. Amon, taking the little King in his arms, acknowledged him as his son and named him his heir.[2] Probably the birth of Amenophis IV had been illustrated in the same way, the same things being said and done, as a testimony to the divine origin of the Pharaoh, and to his right to govern men.

Moreover at this period, at the end of the XVIIIth dynasty, Amon had earned new rights to the grati-

[1] See *ante*, p. 19.
[2] A. Moret, *Du caractère religieux de la royauté pharaonique*, p. 50 *et seq.*

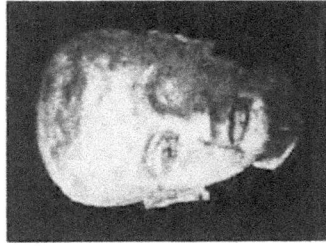

III. A Daughter of Khounaton.
(Berlin).

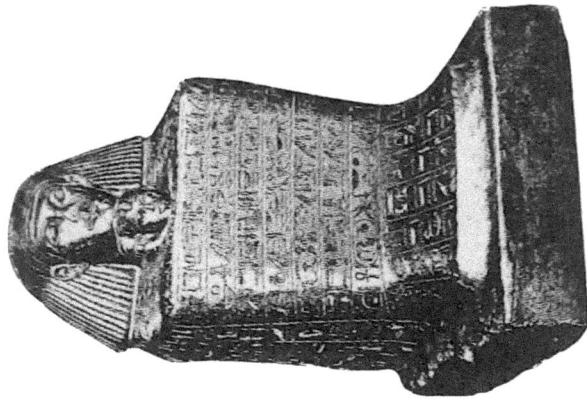

I. Senmout, the Architect of
Deir-el-Bahari.

(Maspero, *Hist.*, *II*, p. 245).

Plate VI.

II. Torso of Young Girl.
(Breasted, *History of Egypt*, Fig. 142).

tude of the kings. It was scarcely two hundred years since the Shepherd Kings, the Hyksos, had come over from Asia and settled in the Delta and in Middle Egypt, subjugating the cities, pillaging the country, and ransacking the temples of the native gods, to enrich with these spoils their own divinities, Baal, the Asiatic, and Soutekhou, the great warrior. Yet owing to the assistance of their patron-god, Amon, the petty Theban kings of the XVIIth dynasty had been able to start upon a war of independence, driving the Shepherd Kings little by little out of Egypt until by the victories of Ahmes I, they were finally expelled. If later, Thotmes I and Thotmes III could conquer the Syrian Ports, traverse the Libyan desert, cross the Orontes, and reach the banks of the Euphrates; if their successors, the Amenophises, established their protectorate over Syria and Palestine in the North, and Nubia in the South, was it not because Amon had continued to fight with Pharaoh and guide the archers and the chariots of Egypt during the battles? The official account of these campaigns, engraved upon the walls of Karnak and Luxor, testify, at least, that these victories were the achievements of Amon, that the conquered lands belonged to Amon, and that the tribute raised in Syria and in Nubia went to swell the treasures of Amon. The Theban god, enriched and strengthened by so many victories, had become the national god, the god of revenge upon the Asiatics.

Father of the Pharaohs, conqueror of the stranger, Amon was, moreover, the god who, through his intermediaries, the priests, upheld the power and authority of the King in the internal government of Egypt. After the glorious reign of Thotmes I, the royal house had been weakened by dynastic quarrels. The Pharaohs had been driven from the throne, supplanted by a woman, the Queen Hatshopsitu; they had been recalled, then banished again; and finally they had been triumphant. The high-priests of Amon had concocted these intrigues, by turn giving and withdrawing their support. They had thus become, in very truth, the governors of the palace, exercising civil authority as well as religious functions. At the time of Hatshopsitu,[1] prince Hâpousenb, under Amenophis III, Phtahmes, held the cumulative offices of "chief prophet of Amon, ruler of all the prophets of the South and of the North, governor of the city of Thebes, vizier of the whole of Egypt."[2] So much spiritual and temporal power,

---

[1] Breasted, *Ancient Records*, II, p. 160. See *ante*, p. 31.

[2] Statuette of Phtahmes, published by Legrain, ap. *Recueil,*

concentrated in one hand, was dangerous in a high degree to Pharaoh! Such ambiguous situations usually end in the servant's taking precedence of his master, ousting him little by little from the government, in order that some fine day, he may himself mount the throne. That is what came to pass some centuries later, at the end of the XXth dynasty, when the priests of Amon became the Pharaohs. This sacerdotal revolution was already in the air at the end of the XVIIIth dynasty; but Amenophis IV was the man who turned aside the natural course of events, breaking the power of the priests of Amon lest they should dethrone the kings. With a far-sighted view of the danger he attempted to overthrow the priesthood of Amon, by doing away, at one and the same time, with the priests and the god.

Was the man who dared thus to measure himself against the mighty Amon one of those exceptional individuals whose giant stature and physical force explain their combative spirit and their power of ruling men? In nowise. Amenophis IV was a man of middle height, of slight build, with round and feminine outlines. The sculptors of the time

---

xxix, p. 83; *cf.* the stela of Lyon, published by Devéria, *Œuvres,* in the *Bibliothèque Égyptologique,* t. iv, p. 84.

have left us faithful portraits of this androgynous body, whose prominent breasts, large hips, and curving thighs present an ambiguous and sickly appearance. The head is very striking with the soft oval of the face, the slightly oblique eyelids, the delicate outline of a long and slender nose, the projeetion of the prominent lower lip, the round and receding skull drooping forward as if the neck were not strong enough to support it (Plate VII, 1). The whole gives the impression of a refined but enervated individual; physically it is a Pharaoh *fin de race.* It has been wondered whether this somewhat degenerate body could be the offspring of two Egyptians of good stock. The mother of the King, Tii, the favourite wife of Amenophis III, was of humble birth; her father, Iouàa, and her mother, Touàa, bore names which have sounded rather Semitic[1] to some scholars, so they thought that Amenophis IV, by his mother Tii, had Semitic blood in his veins, and, as the spirit of his religious reform is strongly monotheistic, this was traced to the direct influence of the maternal blood on the ideas and singular character of the son.[2]

[1] Numerous scarabs that Amenophis had had engraved on the occasion of his marriage with Tii bear the names of his father and mother (*cf.* Maspero, *Histoire,* ii, p. 315). Their names are of true Egyptian origin, as has been proved by Maspero, ap. *Recueil de travaux,* iii, p. 128.

[2] It has been questioned whether Tii was the mother of Ameno-

The soil of Egypt has enabled us to solve this interesting problem. During the month of February, 1905, Mr. Theodore Davis had the good fortune to excavate at Thebes the tomb intact of the father and mother of the Queen Tii. "All the objects which came out of the hypogeum are of the finest Egyptian style, and there is nowhere any trace of foreign influence . . . the mummies themselves afford no positive evidence."[1] Touàa is of the purest Egyptian type; Iouàa has a high-bridged nose, not characteristically Semitic in its curve.[2] It appears from the titles that he bore, that the grandfather of Amenophis IV was a native of Akhmim, a town in the middle of Egypt.

Let us admit that this Reformer-Pharaoh sprang from true Egyptian blood. Moreover, if his physique was somewhat degenerate, his intelligence was not at all so. The religious hymns he composed show him to have been possessed of a mystical mind, with a deep, lively sensibility which

---

phis IV (Wiedemann, ap. *Proceedings*, S. B. A., xvii, p. 156); but letters from the correspondence of El-Amarna designate Amenophis IV as son of Tii (Petrie, *History of Egypt*, ii, p. 209). Concerning this correspondence, see A. Moret, *In the Time of the Pharaohs*, p. 55 *et seq.*

[1] Legrain, *Thèbes et le schisme de Khouniatonou*, p. 13 (ap. *Bessarione*, xi, 1906).

[2] *Cf.* Catalogue du Musée du Caire, *Tomb of Yuaa and Thuia*, 1908, Pl. LVII–LX and frontispiece.

embraced the whole of nature. We know from
the pictures of the times, that he was devoted to
family life; his mother Tïi, his wife, and even his
four daughters appear by his side, not only in the
intimacy of his private apartments, but in all
public functions. . To sum up, Amenophis IV
unites in a hitherto unknown combination the
majesty of the Pharaoh and the virtues of a private
man.   He was kind and simple in manner; he is
a thinker, of subtle mind, persevering and system-
atic; a dreamer and a fanatic, who carries his ideas
to their logical conclusion, and one who did not
shrink from bold measures.

From the beginning of his reign, Amenophis IV
found himself confronted by the god, Amon of
Thebes, whose priesthood had become overbold
by reason of their enormous wealth, and who were
bent upon taming the Pharaohs to their will.
A reaction was necessary and must indeed have
taken place, for in the year 6 of the new reign, a
political revolution, radical in its character, had
been effected.[1]   Thebes was no longer the capital
of Egypt.   The "City of Amon" had become the
"City of Aton"; the high-priest of Amon and the
Amonian priesthood had been swept away, and

[1] Lepsius, *Denkmäler*, iii, 110, b.

the worship of Amon was forbidden throughout Egyptian territory.  Even the name of Amon might not be uttered, it might not be written on stone or on papyrus, and as, in spite of the present, the past still recalled it, engraved on thousands of monuments, the Reformer-King undertook a methodical destruction, not of the monuments, but of the name of the god Amon.  On every wall, on the side of columns, on the summit of obelisks, on the base of tombs, everywhere,—the iconoclasts, commissioned by the King, spied out the cursed hieroglyphics, so that the names of Amon and of the goddess Mout might be ruthlessly hammered out. To erase the name of a god was to slay his soul, [1] to annihilate his double, to destroy his title-deeds, to annul his victories and his conquests.  To suppress Amon was tantamount to rewriting a human history of Egypt, in which the great achievements of the Pharaohs would rightly redound to their honour, and not to that of the arrogant god who called himself their father, but boasted also of being their guide and inspirer.  Finally in order to typify his complete severance from a hated past, the King changed his name of *Amenophis*

[1] *Cf.* Lefébure, *La vertu et la vie du Nom, en Égypte*, ap. *Mélusine*, viii, 10 (1897), pp. 229–231  "The hammering of the name was a veritable murder . . . only the names of people condemned to death, or disgraced were hammered out. . . ."

⌈▭▭▭⌉ to that of ⌈▭▭▭⌉ Khounaton
("he who is liked by the god Aton"[1]).

Probably there was a desperate resistance on the part of the priesthood of Amon, but we possess no particulars of it. Much later, when, after the death of the Reformer-King, the priests of Amon, powerful once more, celebrated the virtues of Toutânkhamon, who restored to them their privileges, they describe the state of Egypt after the revolution in the following terms:

The world was as in the times of chaos, the lands of the gods lay waste from Elephanta to the Delta; their holy shrines were crumbling away and their fields passing into ruin; rank weeds grew therein; the stores were pillaged, and the sacred courts were open to the passers-by. The world was corrupted; the gods were ready to depart, turning their backs upon men, their hearts filled with disgust for their own creatures.[2]

The shadows of this picture are too dark.

---

[1] The meaning of this name (hitherto translated *glory* or *spirit of the god Aton*) has recently been established by Sethe (*Aegyptische Zeitschrift*, xliv, p. 117). M. Schaefer remarks that the King Minephtah Siphtah will take a name constructed on the same plan as *Khounrâ*, "he who is pleasing to Râ." As Sethe states it, *Khounaton* means, with reference to Aton, about the same as Amenophis does with reference to Amon: "Repose, peace of Amon."

[2] Legrain, *La grande stèle de Toutânkhamon*, ap. *Recueil*, xxix, p. 167.

I.  Amenophis IV.—Khounaton.
(Buste du Louvre).

II.  Painted Pavement from the Palace of
El-Amarna.
(Petrie, Tell el-Amarna).

Plate VII.

Where the text says *gods*, we must understand *the god* Amon. The persecution of a single god and of a single form of worship did not imply the ruin of other divinities and other priesthoods.[1] It was against the overwhelming omnipotence of Amon of Thebes that the King had rebelled, trying to supersede him by an older divinity, who had been kept in the background by the dominating Theban god, one, who was less local, but perhaps more familiar and congenial to all, the god *Aton*, whose name now serves to designate the king and the capital of Egypt.

Aton ⵏ̄ is the solar disc; he is the tangible and visible form of Râ the Sun, the oldest perhaps, and the most popular of Egyptian gods. He is represented under the form of a disc, the centre of which is decorated by a raised uræus; the rays of the disc stretch to the earth like arms, terminating in hands; these hands take the offerings from the altars, hold the sign of life to the nostrils of the King, hold him and his kin in their embraces.[2]

---

[1] It is still a disputed question whether or not Khounaton proscribed the worship of other gods than Amon. Breasted remarks that in the tomb of Ramose, and elsewhere, not only has the name of Amon been carefully hammered away, but, also, the word *gods* (*Zeitschrift*, xl, p. 109). See, nevertheless, what is said *post.*, p. 57.

[2] The representation of the radiating disc which is characteristic

In a word, Aton bore the same relationship to
Khounaton as Amon did to Amenophis—a father,
a benefactor, but no longer a tyrannical god.

The King avoids the mistake of reconstituting
for the service of Aton a priesthood on the pattern
of the Theban clergy.   Aton, like Râ, originated
in Heliopolis, so his high-priest bears the same
title (*Our maa*, "chief prophet") as does Râ.   But
the King was careful not to entrust the guardian-
ship of the new worship to the old priestly town
of Heliopolis.   It was in a new town
*Khoutaton*, "the horizon of Aton," the modern
El-Amarna, on the right bank of the Nile, between
Memphis and Thebes, that he laid the foundations
of the temple, with a central obelisk dedicated to
the god Aton.   In Nubia, near to the third cataract,
he built another town Gem-Aton; and in Syria, a
city of which we know not the name.   Both
served in subjugated territories as capitals for the
new state god.   As for the revenues necessary
for the support of the clergy and the god, the King
administered them himself in his capacity of
"prophet-in-chief to Râ-Harmakhis"[1] and "chief

of the monuments of Amenophis IV is nevertheless personal to the
King.  The radiating disc already appeared in the monuments of his
father Amenophis III (Lepsius, *Denkmäler*, iii, 91, g).   After Amenophis IV, the use of this decorative motive disappeared entirely.

[1] Lepsius. *Denkmäler*, iii, 110, *i*.   Harmakhis means Horus
in the horizon.

seer of Aton." This two-fold title is all the more
interesting as it demonstrates the material fusion
of the cults of Harmakhis and of Aton, and the
concentration in the hands of the king of the double
administration of their temporal revenues. We
know, moreover, from a statuette in the Turin
Museum that the relations between the family of
Amenophis IV and the priesthood of Heliopolis
were of long standing. A brother of the Queen
Tii, consequently the uncle of the Reformer, had
been "chief prophet in Heliopolis," and at the
same time "second prophet of Amon."[1]   In the
capacity of heads of the Heliopolitan and Atonian
priesthood, the uncle and nephew administered
the endowments provided for Aton, and the wealth
of Amon that had been confiscated to the service
of Aton. The reform carried out by the King
consists in a secularisation of Amonian property,
a recapture of the lands of the priesthood, and
disestablishment of a state religion to the profit of
another. However towards the end of his reign,
Pharaoh assigned to his most devoted adviser,
Merirâ,[2] the office of high-priest and chief prophet
of Aton[3]; but he was cautious not to bestow upon

[1] L. Borchardt, *Ein Onkel Amenophis III als Hoherpriester von Heliopolis*, ap. *Aegyptische Zeitschrift*, xliv, p. 97.
[2] Breasted, *History*, p. 367
[3] Breasted, *Ancient Records*, ii, p. 405.

him any civil office and limited his powers to the
domain of religion, entrusting to others[1] financial
and judicial administration. The high-priest of
Aton is thus restored to his original position of a
deputy and subordinate of the king. The danger
of his ever becoming a menace to the crown has
passed away.

The Pharaoh not only undertakes the manage-
ment of the estates of the new god, he órganises
the doctrine and formulates the new tenets. The
revolution he has accomplished is not alone political and economical. After having regained the
control of the priesthood and the administration of
church revenues, he becomes the Reformer of the
Faith, and shapes a system of belief according to a
more human ideal.

In order to achieve his aim, the King probably
covered the land of Egypt with temples, dedicated
to Aton. Of these buildings, which were nearly
everywhere destroyed after the death of the King,
there remain scarcely more than a few ruins at
Thebes, Hermonthis, Memphis, Heliopolis;[2] but

---

[1] The most powerful among them was the vizier Ramose
(Breasted, *Ancient Records*, ii, p. 385 *et seq.*) who was not a high-
priest of Aton.

[2] See the texts quoted by Breasted, *Aeygptische Zeitschrift*, xl,
p. 111.

Khoutaton, the capital of the cult of Aton, precisely because it was abandoned by the successors
of the Reformer-King, still exhibits ruins where we
trace palaces and temples,[1] and above all, tombs,
wherein the favourites of Khounaton have represented for us the King in his relations to them.
We see, here, the King, visiting his people, receiv-
ing them in his palace, appearing in the balcony
to throw down to them crowns and necklaces as
tokens of his royal favour, and this favour he
reserves, especially for those "who have hearkened
attentively to his words, and who have understood
and practised his teaching."[2]    In several tombs,
these favourites have, in order to show their
zeal, reproduced verses of the hymns composed by
Pharaoh himself in honour of Aton.    These hymns
are for us texts of a unique and inestimable value.
In translating them, we gain an insight into the large
enthusiastic, mystic mind which conceived such an
exalted ideal as underlies the worship of Aton.

### KHOUNATON'S HYMN.[3]

*Adoration of Harmakhis who rises in the horizon in his*

[1] Petrie, *Tell el Amarna*, 1894; *cf.* Davies, *The Rock-Tombs of El-Amarna*, i–vi, 1902–1908; and Bouriant, Legrain, Jéquier, *Monuments pour servir à l'histoire du culte d'Atonou*, i, 1903.

[2] Breasted, *History*, p. 367.

[3] Breasted, *De hymnis in solem sub rege Amenophide IV conceptis*, 1894.

*name of "Ardour of the solar disc . . .", by King
Khounaton and Queen Nefer-Neferiu-Aton.*

He says:

Thy dawning is beautiful in the horizon of heaven,
O thou, Aton, initiator of life.

When thou risest in the east, thou fillest the earth
with thy beauty; thou art beautiful, sublime, and
exalted above earth. Thy beams envelop the lands
and all thou hast made. As thou art Râ (the creator)
thou conquerest what they give forth, and thou
bindest them with the bonds of thy love. Thou art
afar off, but thy beams are upon (touch) the earth;
when thou art on high, the day follows thy footprints.

*Night:*

When thou settest in the western horizon of heaven,
the world is in darkness like the dead. They lie in
their houses, their heads are wrapt up, their nostrils
stopped, their eyes blind (eye sees not to eye); their
chattels may be robbed even from under their heads,
and they know it not. Then, every lion cometh
forth from his den, every serpent stings, the night is
dark like an oven, the land lies in silence; he who
made them has gone to rest in his horizon.

*Day, Mankind:*

The day breaks, the sky brightens, thou shinest as
Aton in his day; the darkness flees, for thou sendest
forth thy rays, the Two Lands are rejoicing. Men
awake and stand upon their feet, for thou liftest them
up; they bathe their limbs, they take their clothing,
their upraised hands adore thy dawning, the whole
earth is set on her labour.

*Animals:*

The cattle are settled in their pastures, all trees and plants flourish, the birds flutter in the marshes, their wings uplifted in adoration to thy double; all the flocks leap upon their feet;[1] all the birds nestled away, they live, when thou dawnest upon them.

*Waters:*

The ships go forth, both North and South, upon the river, for every highway is open at thy rising; the fishes in the river swim up to greet thee; thy rays pierce the depths of the great sea.

*Men and Animals:*

Thou art he who createst the germ in women. and makest the seed in men, who makest the son to live in the body of his mother and soothest him that he may not cry, and nursest him in his mother's womb, who givest breath to animate all thy creatures.   When the child falleth from the womb, on the day of his birth, thou openest his mouth in speech, thou providest for his needs.

When the chicklet is in the egg, stirring within its shell, thou givest to it breath therein, that it may live. When thou hast made it strong it cometh forth from the egg, chirping its joy to live, and it runneth on its feet when it hath come forth.

How manifold are thy works! Thou didst create the earth in thy heart(when thou wast alone),the earth with peoples, herds, and flocks, all that are upon the earth that go upon their feet, all that are on high, that fly with their wings, the foreign lands, Syria, Nubia, Egypt.[2]

[1] See an illustration of this passage on Plate VIII, 2, of a fragment of pavement in the palace of El-Amarna.

[2] Notice that the King in this enumeration names first the strange countries.   Cf. *post.*, p. 60.

Thou settest every man in his place, creating the things necessary to him; every one has his belongings and possessions; their speech is in diverse tongues, they are varied in form and colour of skin. Thou, the master of choice, madest different (from us) the strange peoples.

Thou createst the Nile in the other world, thou bringest it (upon the earth) at thy desire, to preserve thy people alive . . . thou hast placed a Nile in heaven, that it may fall for them, making lakes upon the hills (great) like the sea; thou waterest the fields among their countries, thou sucklest every, portion of land.

Thou madest the seasons in order to create all thy · works, winter to make cool (thy creatures), summer (to give them warmth). Thou madest the distant heaven that thou mayest rise therein and behold from afar all thou didst make, thou alone. Thou risest in thy form as living Aton, thou breakest forth radiating, shining afar off and returning, thou didst create all the forms through thyself alone, nomes, cities, settlements, roads, and rivers. All eyes behold thee over them, for thou art the Aton, the disc of the day, over the earth.

Thou art in my heart; there is none other that knoweth thee, save me, thy son, Khounaton. . . . O thou by whom, when thou risest, men live, by whom when thou settest, they die, . . . raise them up for thy son, who cometh forth from thy substance, Khounaton.

Every reader of the Hymn of Khounaton will be struck by the lofty inspiration and beauty of expression, for which we have hitherto been used to turn back to no other example than the Bible. It is, perhaps, less fair, to attribute to it the merit of *originality* that the majority of Egyptologists find therein. They admit that the Hymn of Khounaton expresses concepts new in the theological literature of Egypt; the adoration of a god whose epithets are *one*, *only*, all-powerful creator; the expression of a feeling for nature which associates man with the animals, plants, water, and the earth in the worship of the one god, the unique Providence of everything that exists, of everything that has life. These sentiments, even the form of their expression, are they not something quite new in Egypt and do they not date precisely from the time of Khounaton? To answer this question, it would be necessary to possess other hymns, of an earlier date than those of El-Amarna. A comparison of the two texts would enable us to judge of the originality of this one. But the religious poetry before the XVIIIth dynasty is composed—so far as is at present ascertained—only of very short pieces, little hymns graven on funeral stelæ generally addressed to Osiris or to Râ, but owing to limited space, of very circumscribed wording, which does not allow of lyrical development. There is, however, a monument, affording a long hymn of earlier date than

our Hymn of Khounaton. It is a stela preserved
in our French National Library, which, so far,
has never been compared with the texts of El-
Amarna, though it is of high interest. A Hymn
to Osiris was engraved on this stela by order of a
chief overseer of the flocks, Amenemhait, of whose
name the first part *Amen* was hammered out, at the
time when Khounaton caused the name of Amon to
be destroyed wherever it appeared. Chabas, who
has published this stela in a masterly way,[1] con-
cludes: "We ought certainly to consider that this
monument is earlier than Khounaton." The long
Hymn to Osiris, engraved on the stela, proves, first,
that the cult and also the prayers to Osiris, Isis,
Horus, Atoum, Geb,[2] Nouit, gods whose names
have not been hammered out on the stela, have
been respected by the iconoclasts in the pay of
Khounaton. We notice, next, that Osiris is
adored here as the first of the gods, as the creator
of all that exists, earth, water, plants, animals,
men, and gods; as the Supreme Good, the Providence whose care embraces all creatures and extends over every part of the universe. To my mind,
the result of a comparison shows that the religious

---

[1] *Bibliothèque Égyptologique,* ix, p. 95.
[2] *Geb* is the correct reading of the divine name formerly read
*Seb.*

and poetical matter, developed in the hymns of Khounaton, consists of topics already employed in Egyptian literature and probably familiar to every one. "The originality" lent to the hymns of Khounaton is probably like new wine in old bottles; it expresses old beliefs in new rhythms, and gives a touch, as far as we can judge, more vivid and personal to subjects treated by older writers.

It would appear that this point of view is confirmed by other facts. If the hymns are few before the time of Amenophis IV, those which have come to us in later compilations are very numerous. But these hymns, dedicated to Amon, to Thot, to Phtah, reproduce, almost literally a great number of passages characteristic of the hymns to Aton. Like the god of El-Amarna, Amon is called the one and only god, the creator of the earth, water, and animals; he has also with his mighty hand modelled the different races of men, varying in colour and in language. Ought we to conclude that the hymns to Aton even in their most characteristic expressions have been plagiarised by the priests of a rival god, the Theban Amon? If these expressions were peculiar to Atonian literature, it is astonishing that they were not dishonoured and prohibited like the memory of Aton himself. It seems more reasonable to admit that the school of El-Amarna drew its developments from a source that fed both the rival cults. The gods, who successively gained predominance in different historic capitals, were extolled in hymns of the same inspiration, but varying slightly in expression according to the moral standard or intellectual ideal of the period.

This granted, it must be acknowledged that Khounaton grasped these universal topics with uncommon fervidness and developed them into sublime philosophy.

The King's desire seems to have been this: to direct the adoration of the Egyptians towards a god who would not be the artificial creator of a priesthood peculiar to one town, or exclusively national in character, but towards a god incarnating a force in nature, and therefore able to be universally understood and revered.

To this end, the King chose the sun, the primitive god of humanity, whose power, by turn, merciful or pitiless, is nowhere so overwhelming as in the East. This god was no longer presented to men as in former times, under the quaint guise of an heraldic falcon ➤ (Horus or Harmakhis); but as a rayed disc ⨀, the natural manifestation of the divine energy, a hieroglyphic that all men, Egyptians or strangers, even we moderns, could read and understand at first glance.

This god, who personifies motion, light, heat (in his name of "Ardour which is in the Disc"), is verily the benefactor and the giver of life to all that exists. The hymn sets forth with a naïve sincerity, a freshness of expression, and a profusion of images, rushing forth from the depths of primitive emotion, the sentiments of adoration, more or less conscious or confused, which are stirred in men, animals, stones, or plants, when face to face with Him who dispels the night, scares away the wild beasts, fosters the growth of all vegetation, and protects the race of men.

Such sentiments are common to all peoples; but it is perhaps the first time in the history of the world that we see a king calling to the strangers, Semites and Nubians, his newly-conquered subjects, to come and worship, side by side, with his own people, Aton, the Father of All. For the first time, religion is regarded as a *bond* which *binds* together men of different race, language, and colour. The god of Khounaton does not distinguish between Egyptians and Barbarians. All men are equally his sons and should be considered as brothers.

Thus there is at the centre of the universe a

fostering and harmonious Energy which provides for the needs of all living beings, and plays the part of Providence. This energy is Heat and Thought. Such ideas were in the air at this time and there is a text, presumably written at a very ancient date, where the god Phtah, described as Aton is here, is called "the intelligence and the tongue of the gods, source of the thoughts of every god, of every man, and every animal."[1]

This god, with whom the King lives in familiar intercourse, as a child with his father, "whom the King alone—like a prophet inspired by a revelation—is able to understand and make known to men," is a god for all humanity, clothed in a reasonable and beautiful form. Khounaton made him god of the Egyptian Empire at a very opportune moment, when Egypt, extending her conquests beyond her frontiers, incorporates new subjects in Syria and Nubia.

From this point of view, the attempt of Amenophis IV was something more than a political reaction against the encroaching ambition of the high-priests of Amon. The reform of Amenophis IV was at the core a return to a more human form of religion—probably to an archaic ideal which had already flourished in the days of the

[1] Breasted, ap. *Aegyptische Zeitschrift*, xxxix, p. 39 *et seq.*

Ancient Empire, when the god Râ ruled over the gods of the living.

Even as it happened in modern times, this return to a more simple religious sentiment was likewise followed by a renewal in the realm of art. There is a return to a sincere and realistic observation of nature. As the power of his priests increased, Amon became a haughty, distant, unyielding godhead, whose influence affected the Theban artists, on whom devolved the task of decorating the temples and chiselling the statues of the kings. Their art degenerated into stiff solemnity. Their technical mastery is not enlivened by inspiration, and they reflect in bare austere lines the awful majesty of the god. Khounaton, a sincere man, faithful to his ideals, withdrew his favour from this Theban school; he encouraged provincial artists of less skill but more naïve mind, who had remained nearer to nature. As the Pharaoh was in his person and in his acts the habitual theme of the artists, he demanded that he and his family should be represented as they really were, with their physical imperfections, in the intimacy of family life as well as amidst the pomps of the court. Hence these realistic pictures that we find in the tombs of his favourites, where

5

the King appears in familiar attitudes, surrounded by his wife and his daughters, in friendly intercourse with the owners of these tombs. Court festivals, rejoicings over honours conferred upon a faithful servant, ceremonies in the temples, such as the mourning procession led by the King on the death of his beloved daughter Bakitaton—such were the subjects chosen. These subjects were treated by the artists of the Khoutaton School with the same instinct for picturesque 'and lively detail, that freshness and frankness of expression, which shines forth from the hymns analysed above. It was the same spirit which inspired at that period both liturgical poetry and the plastic arts.

It happens that several of these artists exhibit the defects of their qualities. ., Perhaps their technical skill was inferior to the directness of their vision, and they failed to be good artists, while remaining true to nature; several of them have given us portraits of the King and his relatives, which are little less than caricatures. But at least one artist united the realistic tendencies of the new school with the traditions of the pure and classic style of the Thebans. To him, we owe the statue and bust of Amenophis IV (Plate VII, 1), perhaps, also, the head of the little girl, and the torso of a young girl (in all probability

I. Amenophis IV. when Young, and
His Wife.
(Berlin).

II. Khounaton in Later Years, and His
Family.
(Berlin—Spiegelberg, Ægypt, Kunst).

Plate VIII.

one of the royal princesses), works, which by the perfection of their modelling, the accuracy of observation, and the harmonious attainment of life-like execution, rank among the marvels of classical art and of sculpture of all ages.

Amenophis IV reigned scarcely sixteen years, and, perhaps,—if we should judge from certain of his effigies (Plate VIII, 2),— the struggle with the priests of Amon broke down his health and brought upon him a premature old age.   His work did not survive him.   His second successor, Toutânkhamon, son of another wife of Amenophis III, restored the worship of Amon and the power of the high-priests, preparing thus, in a not far distant future (about three hundred years) for the accession of the priest-kings of Thebes.   The temples of Aton were in their turn sacked, and the memory of Khounaton was dishonoured and reviled.   In an official document of the XIXth dynasty, his name is not mentioned; he is designated by a periphrasis: "The fallen one, the criminal of Khoutaton."[1]

The work undertaken by Khounaton had been perhaps premature, at least over-hasty.   Nothing endures without the aid of time.   Khounaton contrived to impart within a few years, to his subjects and to the priests, his fervid faith, the

[1] Loret-Moret, *Inscription de Mes*, ap. *Zeitschrift*, **xxxix, p. 24.**

ardour which consumed his own soul, a reflection of the solar disc. Would and could his reforms survive him? The same question arises with every reformer in history, at the outburst of every revolution. Generally, such sweeping reforms do not last; the stream of the past, dammed up for a moment, the force of tradition, for a moment enchained, return with a formidable rush to submerge the yet unstable work of the revolutionists.

Thus it was with Amenophis IV. Even the new art, momentarily revivified, galvanised into a Renaissance, lapsed again into a stiff and hieratical solemnity

The reform of Amenophis IV hardly affected the development of Egyptian civilisation, but if it counts for little in the history of Egypt, it counts infinitely in the history of humanity. For the first time, perhaps, has man worthily sung his God. And for the first time, in the hymns of El-Amarna, there is expressed with sublime elevation, a feeling of gratitude for a God who is a universal Providence, who extends His care not only to men of diverse races but to animals and plants, a feeling of fraternity with the humblest being in Nature, who, endowed with life, may join in giving forth his praise to his Creator.

# CHAPTER III

## THE PASSION OF OSIRIS

OF all the gods, called into being by the hopes and fears of men who dwelt in times of yore on the banks of the Nile, Osiris was the most popular. His appearance surprises us least of all, when the procession of Egyptian divinities passes before our eyes; this falcon is Horus; this goose, Geb or Amon; that crocodile is Sebek; yonder bull is Hapi, the Nile, and the hippopotamus is Ririt; the pair of lions is Shou and Tafnouit; the vulture and serpent are the goddesses of the South and of the North. Stranger still are those divinities whose human bodies are surmounted by the heads of beasts; from the shoulders of Thot arise the slender neck and the long bill of the ibis; Khnoum wears a ram's head with twisted horns; Sekhit has the terrifying muzzle of a lioness; and Bast carries the head of a cat with ears pricked up and gleaming eyes.

By the side of these animals, fetishes, and totems

of the ancient tribes, raised to the rank of national
divinities in more modern times, there appeared
from the earliest days of United Egypt, a god
whose worship became common to all the cities.
Osiris, in the beginning a multiform fetish, sometimes a tree, sometimes a bull, detaches himself
from his totemic origins and at a very early date
assumes a purely human form. Wherever shone
forth the calm beauty of this face whose oval was
prolonged by the false beard and tall white mitre,
wherever was seen the melancholy outline of this
body, draped in a shroud, the two fists crossed
upon his breast and clasping the ox-herd's whip
and the shepherd's crook, the Egyptians from
every province recognised the "chief" of mankind,
the "Ruler of Eternity," a god who by reason of
his visible shape was nearly akin to man (Plate
IX, 1).

Osiris had lived on earth among men. What
manner of life this had been the priests knew but
did not readily reveal. The hieroglyphic texts
teem with allusions to the events and deeds of the
earthly life of Osiris, but no complete record of
them has come down to us. Is this silence to be
attributed to a mystery surrounding the god
"whose name may not be uttered"? Happily

for us, however, if the Egyptians are silent, the Greeks venerated Osiris no less than the Egyptians, and, in the traditions gathered together by Herodotus, Diodorus, and Plutarch, we are able through the omissions and misunderstandings to form an idea of what the Osirian legend was.

Osiris was son of the god Geb, the Earth, and the goddess Nouit, the Heaven, and he succeeded his father on the throne of the Two Egypts. This was in the time of the divine dynasties. Râ the creator of the world and his descendants, Shou and Geb, had already ruled over men; none of the three had known death, but, overtaken by old age, discouraged by the ingratitude of men, they had withdrawn to the heavens, leaving to a more able god the task of disciplining turbulent humanity. Osiris was the teacher awaited since the creation of the world. When he was born, "a voice proclaimed that the Lord of all things had come upon the earth."[1] A certain Pamyles of Thebes received an "annunciation" of the glad tidings; while going to bring water from the temple of Jupiter (Amon), he heard a voice "which commanded him to proclaim that Osiris, the great

[1] Unless stated to the contrary, that which follows between quotation marks is quoted from the tract *De Iside et Osiride* attributed to Plutarch. "The master of all things" is an Egyptian epithet, *neb r zer.*

king, the benefactor of the whole world, had just been born." By reason of this, the gods entrusted to Pamyles the task of bringing up the child, moulding and preparing him for his high destiny.

Osiris succeeded where his fathers had failed. But he achieved success mainly through the help and magic charms of Isis, h s sister-wife (Plate IX, 2). The divine pair overcame all obstacles by the attraction of beauty, knowledge, and kindness. It was imperative that a ruler should come. Left to themselves by their creator, men lived in savagery, fighting for their food with the wild beasts. Osiris taught them to discern the plants that were good for food—wheat, barley, the vine, which grew in confusion with the other plants. Wondering mankind viewed Isis cutting sheaves of corn and kneading flour. Osiris pressed the grapes, drank the first cup of wine, and where the land was unsuited to the culture of the vine, "he taught the people how to make a fermented drink¹ from barley." Henceforward, men ceased to feed on one another and with cannibalism endemic warfare disappeared.

Men were as yet ignorant of the riches hidden in the earth. Osiris taught them how to find the veins of metal running through the ore; under his

¹ After *Diodorus*, i, 14–16.

I. Osiris, Lord of the Occident.  II.  Isis, the Divine Mother.
(Musée du Caire).

Plate IX.

direction, they worked in gold and brass; "they
made weapons wherewith to slay the wild beasts,
instruments wherewith to cultivate the land, and,
later, statues for the gods." When he had provided men with food and the means of self-defence,
Osiris initiated them into a social and intellectual
life; he gave them a capital, Thebes of the Hundred
Gates; made laws for the community, taught them
ethics and the worship of the gods. In this task,
he had an associate, Thot, the god of the arts
and of letters, who, by the invention of the signs
of speech and writing, made possible the diffusion
of knowledge and the continuance of progress.
Both of them tried to soften manners, and trained
the minds of men by the discipline of the exact
sciences, by the rhythm of games and the arts,
by the cadence of music. At last, men learned to
read the starry sky, acquiring thereby the sense
of a life which went beyond this earthly destiny.

It still remained to carry civilisation to the rest
of mankind. Leaving the government of Egypt
in the hands of his wife, Isis, Osiris gathered together a large army and travelled through the
land, teaching men how to cultivate the cereals.
He rarely had recourse to arms; men came to
him, drawn thither by his speech, spellbound by
the charms of the dance, subdued by music.

Everywhere, Osiris came as a beneficent goa. He was called the "Good Being" (Ounnefer),[1] he who devotes himself to the salvation of all men. Nevertheless, on his return to Egypt, the reward which awaited the benefactor was treachery and death. He fell, not by the jealousy of the gods, like Prometheus, giver of fire; he perished by ingratitude and the spirit of evil.

Side by side with Osiris, lived his brother, the impious Seth-Typhon,[2] even as Evil lives near to Good. Legend relates to us the infernal plot arranged by Seth with the aid of sixty-two accomplices. Seth invited Osiris to a feast at his house.

He had secretly taken the measurements of the figure of Osiris, and had caused to be made a chest of the same size, very richly ornamented; and it was brought into the festal hall. All the guests having examined it with admiration, Seth said to them, as if in jest, that he would present it to any one among them, who, lying down inside it, found he was of the same size. Each having in his turn tried, without its exactly fitting any one of them, Osiris also got in and stretched himself out. Immediately, the conspirators

[1] Perhaps this word originally signified the *Good Hare*, which would be another form of Osiris as a totemic animal.

[2] According to the most recent researches, those of M. Loret, it would follow that Seth or Setesh 𓃝 was, in his totemic form, a wild hare.

ran, closed the chest, and while some nailed down the lid, others poured molten lead along the chinks so that it should be hermetically sealed; after which they carried it to the Nile, whence it was washed out to sea.[1]

As soon as Isis heard of this "great affliction," she cut her hair, clad herself in mourning garb,

ran hither and thither, a prey to the most cruel anguish, asking every one she met concerning the chest for which she was searching; at length she met two little children who had by chance seen the accomplices of Seth pushing the chest into the water and who told her on which branch of the Nile it had happened. The waters had carried the chest to Byblos in Syria, the town of Adonis, where a bush hid it from the eyes. Owing to the virtue of the divine corpse, the bush increased so greatly in size and beauty that its stem enclosed the chest and entirely concealed it from view,[2] until a certain day when Malcandre, the king of the country, cut the stem which hid the chest in its bosom, and made from it one of the columns in his palace.

[1] It was in the locality of Nedit, the site of which is unknown, that Osiris was slain (*Pyramide de Pépi II*, 1, 1263. Cf. *Stèle de Metternich*, 1. 47).

[2] *De Iside et Osiride*, 14–15. Concerning the chest cast into the Nile, *cf.* the magic stelæ of the type of the Metternich stela (published by Golenischeff, 1, 38 *et seq.*) the papyrus of the Louvre, published by Chassinat (*Recueil de travaux*, xiv, p. 14), and perhaps the Harris papyrus (*cf.* Schaefer, *Aegyptische Zeitschrift*, xli, p. 81).

Isis, warned by a heavenly revelation, came to
Byblos. She made herself known, the chest was
restored to her, she took it back to Egypt to the
city of Bouto.[1]

But this only exposed the corpse to fresh out-
rages. "Seth, hunting by moonlight, found the
chest, and having recognised the body of Osiris
cut it into fourteen pieces, which he cast hither
and thither." Isis resumed her mournful quest;
she succeeded in recovering all the fragments of
the corpse save one,[2] which had been cast into the
river, and devoured by an oxyrhynchus. As
Isis found a piece of her husband's body, she
raised a tomb over it upon the very spot, and she
allowed the priests of each of the fourteen sanctuaries to believe that they possessed the whole
body of Osiris.

The woeful "passion"[3] of Osiris ended as his
body found a resting-place in the tomb. But

[1] Seth has shown (ap. *Aegyptische Zeitschrift*, xlv, pp. 12–14)
that the episode of Byblos, the details of which are only known to
us from Greek sources, is yet fundamentally Egyptian in its origin.
*Cf.* Lefébure, *Osiris à Byblos*, ap. *Sphinx*, v–vi. Isidore Lévy,
*Malcandre*, ap. *Revue archéologique*, 1905.

[2] This was the phallus. Note the transposition of this episode
to *The Tale of the Two Brothers* (trans. Maspero, *Les contes populaires de l'Égypte ancienne*, 3e éd., p. 9).

[3] The expression occurs in Herodotus, who speaks of "the
representation of the sufferings of *Him* (Osiris)" τὰ δείκηλα τῶν
παθέων αὐτοῦ, (ii, 171).

divine justice still claimed atonement while mankind repented their ingratitude. Horus, the son of Osiris, with the help of Thot, of Anubis, and of pious men, undertook interminable wars for the purpose of baffling Seth and his allies of their undue heritage of the world. In the end they were victorious. Good triumphed over Evil, and the triumph will endure as long as the descendants of Osiris, gods or Pharaohs, sit upon the "throne of Horus." But will this beneficent existence of Osiris, his final sacrifice for men, be fruitless? Will his passage across the earth be nothing more than the flash of a meteor? This would not conform to the didactic spirit of the popular legends. Let us see how that spirit developed the legend, and what material and moral benefits gods and men derived from the sufferings of Osiris.

Thus far, the gods had not known death. When Râ, the first god-king left the earth for heaven, his white hairs, his dribbling mouth, his trembling limbs, witnessed to his decrepitude. But, in the case of the gods, old age did not lead to death. The murder of Osiris by Seth revealed to them that they were not invulnerable to the attacks of another god; at the first contest between the sons of Râ, at a fresh attack of evil, the gods would be confronted, like Osiris, with the hideous fatality of death. How might this danger be avoided? There would be no safety for them till their master in knowledge, Osiris, should be restored to life.

Isis, the companion and inspiration of the dead god, his sister Nephthys, Thot and Anubis, who shared his thoughts, Horus, his beloved son, who had inherited his wisdom, found in the teachings of Osiris himself, the secret which would recall him to a new life and a better one—that would make him invulnerable to a second death. Plutarch explains and sums up the Osirian knowledge in these short words: "Isis invented the remedy which confers immortality." In fact, she succeeded in transforming the corpse of Osiris into a resuscitated god, by the invention of magic funeral rites.

Such rites as had been instituted by Isis, "the first time," were performed at the great festivals of Osiris and of the dead. The most important were celebrated at the beginning of winter, from the 12th to the 30th Choïak, in sixteen of the large towns of Egypt.[1]  At Sais, Herodotus saw "the Egyptians perform by night the representation

[1] V. Loret, *Les Fêtes d'Osiris au mois de Choïak,* ap. *Recueil de travaux relatifs à l'archéologie et à la philologie égyptiennes,* t. iii–v.

of the sufferings undergone by *Him;* they called them the Mysteries." It was a sacred drama, played by the priests and priestesses before all the people, who took part in the events of the action. But Herodotus reveals nothing of what he has seen: "Upon these Mysteries, all of which, without exception, are known to me, let my lips guard a religious silence!"[1] I shall now attempt to give a general idea of these Osirian rites, as it can be gathered from the texts in the tombs and the temples.

The opening scene represented the death of the god. Some imitation was made of dismembering a body and scattering its fragments abroad. Then Isis set out on her *quest;* "she *sought* Osiris without ceasing; she wandered to and fro, lamenting, and rested not till she had *found* him."[2] Horus, the son of the dead king, Thot and Anubis, his friends, take part in the "quest"; the episodes of which are summarised in the sacramental words quoted by Herodotus.

When Osiris had been found, the play proceeded to bring together his dismembered body. Diodorus relates how Isis restored to life each member

---

[1] Herodotus, ii, 170, *cf.* ii, 62. See C. Sourdille, *Hérodote et la religion de l'Égypte*, p. 67.

[2] *Stèle de la Bibliothèque nationale* (*Hymne à Osiris* ll. 14-15).

of the mutilated god, as it was recovered. "She enclosed each fragment in a life-size effigy of Osiris, made of wax and perfumes." This suggests a magic process, the first step of which is to fashion an image of Osiris. The fictitious body, on contact with the piece of flesh placed within it, was supposed to become alive, according to magic creed. After these brief and partial obsequies, the family of Osiris effected in detail an entire reconstruction of the divine body. The Rituals[1] state that Horus made for Osiris a large statue (we would term it a "mummy") by joining together all the parts that Seth had severed. "Thou hast taken back thy head," say Isis and Nephthys to their brother; "thou hast bound up thy flesh; thy vessels have been given back to thee; thou hast regained thy members." The gods take part in this difficult operation. Geb, the father of Osiris, presides over the ceremony; Râ sends from heaven the goddesses Hawk and Uræus, those who encircle like a crown the forehead of the gods, "in order to put the head of Osiris in its place and to join it to his neck."

The description we read in the Rituals was carried out faithfully in practice. At the solemn festivals of Osiris, two complete statues of the

[1] A. Moret, *Rituel du culte divin*, pp. 74-75.

Funeral Vigil of Osiris   Ounnefer Dead.
(Abydos, temple de Séti I).

god were fashioned from earth mingled with wheat,
incense, perfumes, and precious stones; but the
fragment of the body assigned by Isis to each
sanctuary was fashioned apart, and when the
priest brought the clay to pour it into the mould,
he recited these words: "I bring to Isis these
fragments of the mummy of Osiris."

Near to the statue, now clad in the clinging
shroud which will henceforth be the characteristic
garb of Osiris, Isis and Nephthys, in mourning
robes, their hair unbound, their head and breast
bruised with repeated blows, intone a kind of
*vocero*, a funeral dirge. They implore Osiris
"to return to inhabit his reconstituted body"[1]
(Plate X).

"Come to thy dwelling," says Isis, embracing
the feet of the mummy.

Thine enemies are not here. Come to thy dwelling!
Look at me! It is I, thy sister, whom thou lovest, do
not withdraw thyself from me. Come to thy house
even now! When I see thee no longer, my heart
laments for thee, my eyes search for thee, I run to and
fro, seeking to find thee. Come to her who loves thee,
Ounnefer, come to thy sister, come to thy wife; O

[1] The text has been published by J. de Horrack under the title:
*Les Lamentations d'Isis et Nephthys.* The scene where Isis and
Nephthys *recover* Osiris is described in the texts of the Pyramids
(*Pépi*, I, 1, 475 *et seq.;* édit. Sethe, formule 532).

6

thou whose heart no longer beats, come to thy dwelling; I am thy sister, born of thy mother, do not leave me; the gods and men all together weep for thee; and I, I call thee, raising my voice as high as the heavens. . . . Dost thou not hear my voice? It is I, thy sister, whom thou didst love on earth, and thou lovest none more than me.

And Nephthys, who guards the head of the mummy, begins the next strophe:

O fair prince, come to thy dwelling to rejoice thy heart; none of thine enemies is here; we are thy two sisters who are at thy side to guard thy funeral bed and to call thee with tears; turn thyself upon thy bed to look upon thy sisters. . . . Thine enemies are overcome. Here am I with thee in order to protect thy limbs. . . . Come to see thy son Horus, king of the gods and men; he performs the rites for thee. Thot pronounces the incantations, he calls thee with the right formulæ; the children of Horus guard thy flesh. . . . Thy soul receives the rites every day; the gods, bearing the sacred vases, come to refresh thy double. Come to thy sisters, our prince, our lord. Withdraw thyself no longer from us.

These lamentations of Isis and Nephthys express naïvely an idea common to all popular languages. After death, Osiris goes away, far from his body, far from his house, far from his family. In order to bring him back to his corporeal remains, he must be reassured, promised security, cajoled with kind words. Thus entreated, he

returns at last to the fictitious body, modelled
by Horus.

The second act, as it were, of the drama thus
played, consists of the following scenes: The
return of the soul of Osiris and the resurrection of
the god. In order that Osiris should be reborn,
it was necessary, by magic rites, to *imitate* the
phenomena of life, or to simulate the rebirth.
There were two ways of illustrating the rebirth of
Osiris—either to imitate in magic rites the return
of activity in the body or to simulate delivery.
In certain temples, the statue was placed for seven
days upon branches of sycamores. The explanation appended to the sacred texts declares that this
was intended to recall the *seven* months passed by
Osiris in the womb of his mother Nouit, the goddess
of the sycamore. "One day counts for a month,
the sycamores are for Nouit." According to the
laws of imitative magic, this gestation or this
simulated delivery, assures to the statue a veritable
rebirth. Some days later, the statue, made, as
has been said, of mould, barley, wheat, perfumes,
was buried under the holy sycamores, on the day
of the Feast of the Fields, that is, at seedtime.
Some months later, the barley and the wheat will
spring up upon the statue of Osiris. The sym-

bolism speaks for itself; the god returns to life at the same time as the vegetation.[1]

The priests endeavoured to give a still more precise picture of the mysteries which occurred in the bosom of the earth. At Denderah and Philæ[2] are bas-reliefs which describe the phases of the resurrection of Osiris. At first, we see the corpse stretched upon a funeral bed with its face

FIG. 7.—Isis and Nephthys Resuscitating Osiris.
(From Georges Bénédite, *Le Temple de Philæ*, pl. xl.)

to the sky.   Isis and Nephthys, the two goddesses, seem to be brooding over the corpse; their hands urge on the recreation of the new skeleton; one after the other, the legs, the body, the head appear in answer to the call of the magnetic passes.   At last, the god seems resuscitated; he turns suddenly upon his side, lifts his hand to his face, and raises his head, smiling (Fig. 7).   Farther on, another

[1] V. Loret, *Les Fêtes d'Osiris au mois de Choïak*.
[2] Mariette, *Denderah*, t. iv, Bénédite, *Philæ*.

picture presents the symbolic plant-growth of Osiris. The mummy is lying down; a priest sprinkles it with water, and from the body, thick and tall, spring the new ears of grain. "This," says the legend, "is the form of Him whose name may not be uttered (Osiris), springing from the water which renews his life"[1] (Fig. 8).

The lapse of time required for illustrating resurrection by plant-growth made the practice of these rites inconvenient. The Osirian rebirth by germination called for months, the time essential for the sprouting of the seeds. So the celebration of those Mysteries was confined to the great annual fêtes. In daily practice, it was necessary to have recourse to summary and potent rites, in order to bring about an instantaneous resurrection of the dismembered god.

This was effected by simulating, side by side with the vegetable an animal rebirth. A victim was sacrificed and its life taken, in order that this life escaping from the body of the victim might enter the body of Osiris. Sometimes the victims were men, prisoners of war, Libyans with red hair, recalling the image of Seth, who had red skin and

[1] Chambers of Osiris at Philæ (Lanzone, *Dizionario di mitologia Egizia*, Pl. CCLXI, and G. Bénédite, *Le temple de Philæ*, Pl. XL).

hair; but usually a bull, a gazelle, or some horned animal, sacred to Seth, was sufficient. After slaughtering the animal, Horus seized the statue of Osiris and laid it down in the skin of the beast; likewise, on the eve of the funerals, a priest would lay himself down in the bloody shroud as a proxy for the dead. This was called "the rites of good burial in the hide of Seth."[1] Diodorus relates a variant upon this rite. "Isis gathered together the scattered members of Osiris and enclosed them in a wooden cow."[2] Here is imitated the gestation, followed by delivery, indispensable preliminaries to the new life promised to Osiris. (Even to-day, in India, when a man has been contaminated by contact with infidels, he believes he can be reborn, purified, if he passes through a golden cow in order to simulate birth.[3]) A chant, recited by Horus, sums up the meanings of these rites: "I

[1] See the texts quoted by A. Moret, *Du sacrifice en Égypte*, in the *Revue de l'histoire des religions*, January, 1908.

[2] I, 85. Herodotus (ii, 129 and 132) relates also that at the festival of Osiris, there was exposed a cow of gilded wood in which the King Mycerinus had enclosed the body of his dead daughter. This cow was evidently an object appertaining to funeral rites. The text of Denderah describes in detail "the cow of sycamore wood, covered with linen, in which was placed the mummy of the god" (*Recueil*, iv, p. 26). The god was born anew like the Sun, who, under the form of a calf, comes forth from the womb of Nouit, the goddess-cow of the heavens. (*Cf.* A. Moret, *Rituel du culte divin*, p. 208.)

[3] Frazer, *Le Totémisme*, p. 48; Lefébure, *Sphinx*, viii, p. 47.

am Horus, who moulded his father, Osiris; I fashion him who fashioned me; I cause to be born him who caused me to be born; I call into life the name (that is, the personality) of him who begat me."[1]

The soul had not returned into this revivified form. According to the legend, the soul of Osiris, after the cruel mutilation of his body, had taken its flight to the moon.[2] Among certain savage races, the belief is still to be found, that the souls of the dead reside in the moon. Osiris's soul followed the changes of the luminary, which each month decreases, wanes, disappears, in order to be reborn and to increase in size at the beginning of the following month. The Egyptians explained these vicissitudes thus: Seth, the implacable enemy of Osiris, disguising himself as a black pig, or some other animal, attacked, on the fifteenth day of each month, the luminary laden with souls, and gradually devoured it and all it contained. It was the duty of Horus and Thot to set out to hunt, to undertake the "sacred quest" and to capture pig, bull, gazelle, or goose devoted to Seth; once the animal was caught, Horus cut his neck and made him "disgorge what he had eaten," and

[1] A. Moret, *Rituel du culte divin*, p. 223, no. 2.
[2] *Ibid.*, p. 112. *Cf.* P. Pierret, *Études égyptologiques*, p. 87.

triumphantly "took back to Osiris the recovered soul."

Bringing the head, the heart, and the thigh of his victim close to the mouth of Osiris, Horus said to his father: "I have led thy adversaries to thee; I have cut off such a part from the victim: thy soul is within it." The statue thus recalled to life, still remained motionless; Horus pressed with his fingers, or touched with ritual instruments, the mouth, the eyes, the ears, and various parts of the body, imitating the movements proper to each organ, restoring to Osiris the use of his eyes to see with, his ears to hear with, his mouth to eat and talk with, his hands to work with, and his legs to walk with. The formulæ necessary for the performance of this imitative magic had been preserved in books of ritual, entitled *Books of the Opening of the Mouth*" (*àp-ro*).[1] This recall to life was strengthened by embraces and magnetic passes: the "fluid of life," transmitted from Horus to Osiris, returned from the father to the son.

The life now restored to the new body of Osiris must be preserved. Hence, a series of new scenes —a third act—in the sacred drama. The statue was given into the hands of the dressers, and submitted to a very elaborate toilet, in which ablutions,

[1] A. Moret, *In the Time of the Pharaohs*, p. 197.

fumigations, incensing, anointing with paint, were all operations having a magic significance. Afterwards, the statue was swathed in bandages, adorned with necklaces, weapons, and crowns, and everything was calculated—the texture and colour of the fabrics, of the metals, or of the precious stones—to produce the maximum of magical effect against the enemy, Seth. Then the god was placed before a table laden with "all things good and pure that heaven gives, that earth creates, that the Nile yields from her stores." The menu as given included breads, meats, fruits, and various drinks and removed for ever all fear of thirst or hunger.

Finally, the statue, well-fed, was laid in a shrine, the doors of which were sealed and bolted.[1]

Henceforward Osiris lived a new life, which he was the first to know.

In this second existence, Osiris remained king of the Two-Egypts, but his dwelling was in heaven; he performed all the acts of his first life, but without growing old; he enjoyed an ideal existence which was not to be ended by a second death. The rites which had resuscitated Osiris had made him immune against the attacks of Seth.

[1] H. Junker, *Die Stundenwachen i. d. Osirismysterien*, 1910.

Horus and likewise men, by rehearsing the Osirian ceremonies every day assured to their benefactor that continuance of second youth, which had not been enjoyed either by Râ, the demiurge, or by his successors, Shou and Geb, who, without dying, had been subject to senile decay.    Death, as Osiris had known it, was henceforward desirable to gods and men; it opened to them the gates of a renewed existence and led to immortality.

As the life of Osiris had been beneficent, so his death saved men from final annihilation.    In this sense, the "passion" of Osiris became a "redemption" of gods and men.

As far back as the Ancient Empire, we see that all the gods receive the rites of the Osirian cult. The relatives and allies of Osiris, Horus, Isis, Thot, Anubis; his ancestors, Râ, Geb, Shou; the other gods of earth and heaven,—accept a mortal fate in order to baffle destruction by Seth and to enter into a life of eternal splendour.    The purpose of the cult for them is to place them in the same conditions in which Osiris had been.    The formulæ of the holy service reveal to us that every god adored in the temple is supposed to have been killed, dismembered, bereft of his soul by Seth. This explains why the religious texts allude to the tombs of the gods, a statement supported by Greek tradition: "The priests of Egypt say, not only of Osiris, but in general of all the gods, that their bodies rest among them, buried and honoured, while their souls are shining stars in the sky."[1]

But the Greek author omits to say that the rites of resurrection were repeated for the benefit of the buried gods. Why should not the formulæ which had proved so miraculously efficient for Osiris exercise the same virtue when applied to the other gods? The result was that any god assimilated to the Good Being was also called an Osiris, though he retained at the same time his own personality, attributes, and particular characteristics.

From the gods, redemption was then extended to men: the cult of the dead rested on the same identification with Osiris as the worship of the gods. It was but "the representation of the divine mystery which had formerly been accomplished upon Osiris."[2] That is why every dead person was called *Osiris Such-and-such-a-one;* the deceased is supposed to have been dismembered, then restored; his son assumes, while celebrating the cult of his parent, the name of Horus, and the widow of the deceased, the name of Isis. In the same way, the friends of the family play the parts

---

[1] *De Iside et Osiride,* 21.
[2] G. Maspero, *Études de Mythologie,* i, p. 291.

of Thot and Anubis.   The king, who is the son
and heir of the gods, when he performs the worship
of the gods, is called Horus.   Thus, the State

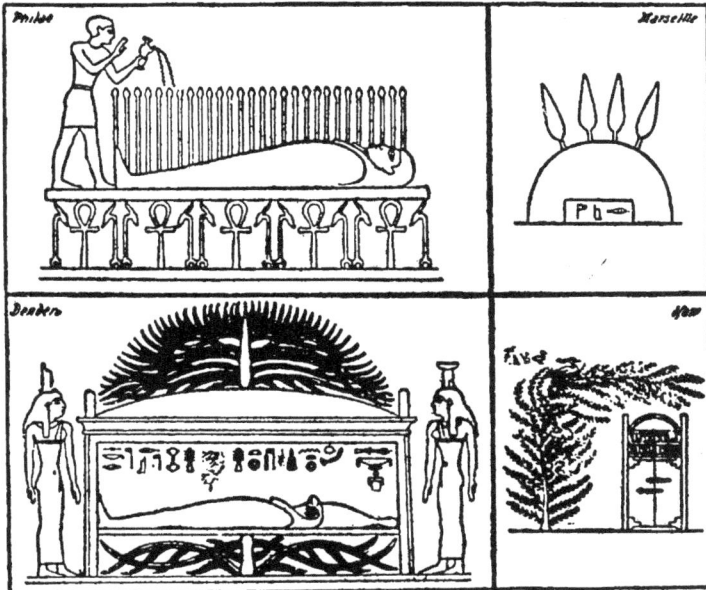

FIG. 8.—Four Representations of the Tomb of Osiris.
(From E. Meyer, *Ægypten zur Zeit der Pyramidenbauer.*)

   1.—*Philae.*   The priest offers up a libation of water " which renews the
life of Osiris."   Twenty-eight ears of corn grow on the divine body.
   2.—*Denderah.*   Tomb of Sokaris-Osiris, guarded by Isis and Nephthys.
A tree springs from the body of the god.
   3.—Sarcophagus of *Marseille.*   The mound (*ouârit*) where Osiris was
buried.   Four trees shade it.
   4.—*How.*   Picture of a sarcophagus.   The soul of Osiris, in the shape of
a bird, alights upon the tree growing from the tomb.

worship, celebrated by the king, the private
worship, celebrated by each individual for his
dead relatives, are based upon the Osirian rites.
The festival of Osiris became the festival of all

the dead. At the festivals of Bubastis, all the people took part in the mourning for Isis, and "each one smote himself" to show his grief. At Sais, as is further stated by Herodotus, the lamps were lighted in the evening when the passion of Osiris was commemorated; those lights, throughout all Egypt, associated in this commemoration the ancestors of each house with the ancestor of all, who had been the first to overcome death.[1] These popular festivals may be compared to the Mysteries of the Passion in the Middle Ages or the sacred festivals still to be seen at Oberammergau. In Egypt, as with us, the cradle of dramatic poetry was the temples.[2]

Of each dead man and of each god who enjoys new life through Osirian resurrection the texts say that we shall see "his name bloom again"[3] as blooms the sacred tree,[4] or as the ears of corn grow on the body of Osiris. In fact, grains of

---

[1] Herodotus, ii, 61–62, 170–171.

[2] A. Wiedemann, *Die Anfänge dramatischer Poesie im alten Aegypten*, 1905.

[3] This is the title of numerous funeral papyri. An edition has been issued by Lieblein: "*The book that my name may blossom*."

[4] The tomb of Osiris is generally shaded by trees, which prove by their vitality the resurrection of the god. *Cf.* H. Schaefer, *Das Osirisgrab von Abydos und der Baumpeker* (*A. Z.*, xli, p. 107). See Fig. 8.

wheat or barley were often slipped in with the
corpse, so that their germination in the earth
might urge on the rebirth of the dead man.   In
a tomb of the XVIIIth dynasty, the resurrection
was represented in this way:

"A canvas is stretched above a rush mat upon a
framework of wood.   In the middle of the canvas
an outline of Osiris haṣ been traced in ink," then
this enclosed portion has been covered with soil
and sand sown with barley-seed.   After the grains
have germinated and have reached a height of
eight centimetres, the stalks have been clipped
"and a kind of green carpet in the shape of Osiris
has been obtained"[1] (Plate XI).

Thus, then, gods and men, who during their
lives are as far apart as the heaven is from the
earth, become united after death by the Osirian
rites, by an assimilation with the Good Being
who played the part of a victim.   We have seen
that at the beginning of the divine service, the
god or the man to whom worship is offered is
supposed to have been put to death and mutilated,
just as Osiris had been.   This explains why in the
tombs of prehistoric Egypt, we find corpses dismembered, according to the Osirian rite.   Now,

[1] Daressy, *Fouilles dans la vallée des Rois*, i, p. 26.

primitive people admit that like produces like; a
magician by mutilating a waxen image is able,
by the laws of magic, to wound and kill from afar
the original of the image. To repeat upon the
corpse of a man the mutilations formerly suffered
by Osiris, is to act directly upon the god himself;
to dismember a holy statue of Osiris is to dismember the god anew. As often as worship is
offered, that is, at every repetition of the Osirian
rite, there is inflicted upon the Good Being a
renewal of his suffering. At every bloody mystery
accomplished in any tomb or temple, on behalf
of a man or a god, Osiris again undergoes his
passion, death, and rebirth. He is sacrificed on
every altar.

How far is this sacrifice conscious and voluntary?
How far does Osiris offer up himself for the redemption of mankind? It does not seem probable that
in primitive times the divine victim offered himself
in sublime abnegation to be sacrificed; the oldest
conception is rather of a passive victim, overcome
by the force of magic rites. But even as far back
as the time of the Pyramids, the texts indicate
progress in the moral attitude of Osiris.

We have seen, that in order to restore life to the
corpse of the god, the life of a sacrificed animal
had to be transferred to it. This was, oftenest an

animal sacred to Seth, so naturally the *enemy*[1] of
Osiris.  Here an interesting point arises.  The bull,
the gazelle, the goose, once the priest has decapi-
tated and dismembered them, are in the same
state as that in which Osiris had been placed
by Seth, whence he had entered upon immortality.  Henceforward, and still by virtue of
imitative magic, the sacrificed victim loses its hostile character.  By the Osirian death, the victim
is sanctified and redeemed; its soul, freed from its
body after the mutilation, may soar to the world of
the Osirian gods.  Seth and Osiris, the victim and
the god, are no longer to be distinguished one from
the other, but are joined in a common immortality.

These subtle speculations are found fully
developed in other religions; for instance, in the
Vedic rituals.  They are obscurely set forth in
the Egyptian texts.  The bull, supporter of Seth,
adversary of Osiris and sacrificed as such, becomes
the agent by which Osiris is conveyed to heaven.
He bears him on his back, or lends his hide wherewith to make a sail for the divine barge sailing
to Paradise.  In fact, the typhonian animal
becomes the saviour, the liberator, the father of
the de d man or god: "Thy father is not among

[1] This is the original meaning of our word host (from *hostis,*
enemy).

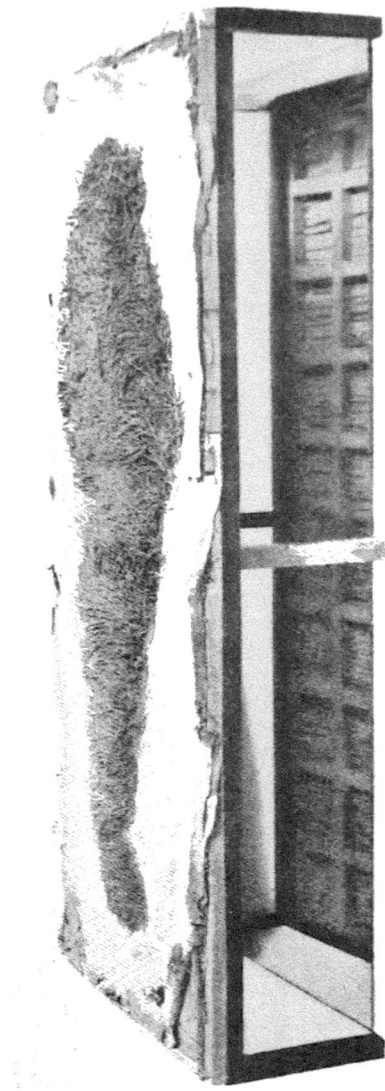

The Dead Resurrected in the Form of a Sprouting Osiris.
(Musée du Caire).
Plate XI.

men; thy father is th. great victim [the bull]."
Osiris even becomes confused with the bull:
"Thou art the bull of the sacrifice."[1]

If I understand rightly the meaning of facts
and texts which are difficult of interpretation,
we are now far away from the conception of
primitive times in which the part taken by Osiris
in the cult was somewhat automatic and passive.
Here, the Redeemer appears to extend to his
adversary the benefit of his sufferings; he draws
along with him into the way of salvation the
enemy from whom he can no longer be separated,
since Evil was the cause of Good.  Without Seth,
the murderer, could men have known Osiris, the
Redeemer?

This interpretation provides the key to other
obscure passages of the Rituals.  After the bloody
sacrifice, a supper is served to Osiris, or to the
divine or human beings, objects of the worship.
The liquid or solid offerings—bread, fruits, wines,
milk, and butter, which are presented to the god,
bear the mystical name of the "Eye of Horus."
This means they are the offspring of the son of
Osiris, his progeny, his flesh, for according to
Egyptian metaphysics the god brings forth into

[1] See the texts quoted by Lefébure, *ap.* A. Moret, *Du sacrifice
en Égypte.*

7

reality everything that he names and that he *sees.*[1] That which is offered to Osiris—or to the Osirian gods who receive the same worship—is his own body and blood, which the god divides among the priests and relatives, under the appearances of liquid and solid offerings. This holy food partaken of in common, this holy communion, makes clergy and worshippers together participants in the blessings of his passion and sacrifice.

The Holy Writings contain rather suggestive passages on these points: "Osiris knows the day when he shall pass out." Does not this foreboding imply that the god is resigned to his agony and obedient unto Death? "The heart of Osiris is in every sacrifice, . . ." which is no less expressive of the voluntary, daily immolation of the god.[2] "Thou art the father and the mother of men; they live upon thy breath; they eat the flesh of thy body[3] . . ." a forcible commentary on one of the epithets of Osiris, "the great victim."

---

[1] The Egyptians believed that man and all matter were emitted from the divine eye of Râ, *i.e.*, proceeded from Light. Nothing existed in the Universe until the Creator Râ *saw* beings and things and *named* them. *Cf.* A Moret, *In the Time of the Pharaohs*, p. 243.

[2] *Livre des Morts*, xvii. E. de Rougé, *Études sur le rituel funéraire*, ap. *Revue archéologique*, June 1, 1860, p. 345; *cf.* Éd. Naville, *Das aegyptische Todtenbuch*, Varianten, p. 65.

[3] Ostracon du Caire, pub. by Erman (*Aegyptische Zeitschrift*, 1900, pp. 30–33).

I have attempted to draw the line between what is human and what is supernatural in the life and death of Osiris; it remains to find a satisfactory explanation of his fate. Whence arose the conception of a sublime hero, a benefactor of men, who, betrayed by his brother and his people, found in death the weapon wherewith to overcome death, who, far from taking revenge upon his executioners, made them benefit by his sufferings and delivered the world from the terror of the hereafter?

The Greeks found nothing absurd nor purely fabulous at the root of the Egyptian myths; "their myths can all be explained by moral or practical reasons, or else they recall interesting historical events or refer to some natural phenomena."[1]

The author of the treatise *De Iside et Osiride* enlightens us upon the interpretations of the Osirian myth given by the Ancients. Some thinkers would discover therein "the memory of certain kings, to whom, as owing to their exceptional virtue and power, a divine origin was attributed, and who afterwards fell into great misfortunes." Plutarch contemptuously dismisses this explanation as impious, because it degrades the gods to the rank of mortals; he also scoffs at

[1] *De Iside et Osiride*, 8.

Evemerus of Messina, for whom the divine heroes are but kings and chieftains who lived in olden times. "When you hear all the fables that the Egyptians relate concerning the gods, when you are told that they wandered upon earth, were cut in pieces, and that they experienced many other similar accidénts, do not imagine that all that really happened."[1]   Modern criticism is less absolute.   We do not admit with M. Amélineau that the real tombs of Horus and of Seth, or the shrine of Osiris, have been discovered in prehistoric Abydos.   Nevertheless, other scholars, like Professor Frazer, working independently in other domains, have traced in primitive kingship, or in the customs of savage tribes of to-day, some of the features that characterise the legend of Osiris. Often enough, a primitive or savage king is treated, living or dead, as an expiatory victim;[2] his body, beheaded and dismembered, is scattered abroad upon the land, in order to ensure magic protection, and fertility of the soil.

While rejecting the Evemeristic explanation of legends, Plutarch admits that, in the case of Osiris, it rested "upon true facts and real accidents";

---

[1] *De Iside et Osiride*, 11.
[2] J. Frazer, *Adonis Attis Osiris*, p. 277; *Lectures on the Early History of the Kingship*, p. 253.

but, he adds, "it is one of those dogmas which is
so wrapped about with fable and allegory that we
can only see faint traces of truth glimmering in
darkness." The Egyptian priests, he further
states, made use of "enigmatic and mysterious
language and enveloped the dogmas in a veil of
allegory."[1] What meanings then can we discover
beneath the myth of Osiris? Plutarch's answers
are varied and sometimes contradictory.

He first tells us that among the Ancients "Osiris
personified the Nile, which unites itself with Isis,
the land; that Seth-Typhon is the sea in which the
Nile loses itself by many branches; that the
Egyptian priests hold the sea in horror and call
the salt in it Seth's scum. The greatest philosophers among the priests add that Osiris is the
human principle, the source of all production, the
substance of all germinating things; that Seth-
Typhon, on the contrary is the principle of heat
in fire, the cause of drought, the enemy of moisture.
. . . The snares that Typhon spreads for Osiris
typify the terrible effects of drought when it
absorbs the moisture of the Nile . . .; the body
of Osiris, enclosed in a chest, means nothing more
nor less than the diminishing and the disappear-
ance of the waters of the Nile. Horus, in the end,

[1] *De Iside et Osiride*, 20, 9–10.

triumphs over Seth; that is to say, that after the rise of the Nile, the inundation[1] of its waters will again replenish the earth." There seems to be some truth in these explanations, M. Maspero has, in fact, proved that Osiris was first worshipped in the Delta, and especially at Busiris and Mendes.[2]

Several Greek commentators added to this physical symbolism an interpretation derived from astronomy. "Typhon represents the solar world; Osiris, the lunar; the moon, which gives the nightly dews, the principle of moisture and fruit-fulness, stimulates the generation of animals and the growth of plants; the sun, on the contrary, burns up the earth with its fire and withers it." In support of their arguments, a great number of facts could be quoted, which meet with the consideration of the modern critic.[3] Osiris lived or reigned twenty-eight years; this is about the length (to be exact, twenty-nine and a half days) of the monthly course of the moon. The death of Osiris

[1] *De Iside et Osiride*, 32–33, 39–40.

[2] The aspect of the inundated plains of the Delta, of the river which washes and fertilises them, of the desert sand that menaces them, inspired the theologians of Mendes and Bouto with an explanation of the mystery of the creation in which the gods of these cities, Osiris, Seth, Isis, filled the chief parts. See G. Maspero, *Histoire*, i, pp. 129–135. *Cf.* Ed. Meyer, ap. *Aeg. Zeitschrift*, xli, p. 97.

[3] *De Iside*, 41. *Cf.* Frazer, *Adonis Attis Osiris*, p. 359 *et seq.*

occurred on the seventeenth day of the month, the day when the full moon begins to wane; Seth divided the body into fourteen pieces (according to the most ancient tradition); this is exactly the number of days during which the moon decreases and finally disappears. At the beginning of the month, Osiris enters into the new moon. "His soul," said a text, "rejuvenates in the moon on its first day." The festival calendars found in the temples confirm Plutarch's statements; Osiris was worshipped especially on the second, the sixth (first quarter), the fifteenth of the month (full moon);[1] on this day of the expected, inevitable catastrophe to which Osiris must succumb, there was sacrificed, as if to retard the "great affliction," a black pig, one of Seth's animals that swallowed the lunar disc. During the last days of the month, from the 17th or 20th Athyr, according to some, from the 16th to the 30th Choïak, according to others,[2] the death and resurrection of Osiris were celebrated. At the time when the corpse of the god was supposed to have been recovered from

---

[1] A. Moret, *Rituel du culte divin*, p. 97.

[2] The festivals were celebrated in the month of Choïak during the Ptolemaic period; in the month of Athyr, according to Plutarch, at the end of the first century of the Christian era. See, on this subject, J. Frazer, *Adonis Attis Osiris*, p. 325 *et seq.* The 19th Athyr would correspond to the 15th of November.

the Nile, the priests moulded a little image in the form of a new moon.[1]

Whether Osiris was the beneficent Nile or the fertilising moon does not yet explain how his death became for men "the bread of life" and secured them immortality. So Plutarch was not at fault when he said: "Each of these explanations in particular is false, but taken together they are true," in the sense that they each show one side of the problem. But Plutarch goes on to relieve his mind of another hypothesis to which he gives no credit: "They say that Osiris is buried when the seed is sown in the ground, that he returns to life when the plants begin to sprout."[2]

This explanation seems absurd to the author of *De Iside et Osiride;* it is nevertheless the one that I the most readily admit. Agricultural peoples, in a primitive state of society, attribute to spirits the changes of the seasons, the periodical fertility of the earth, as well as the annual death of vegetation. The fields, they say, are peopled with spirits who sleep in winter, awake in springtime,

---

[1] *De Iside et Osiride,* 39.

[2] *De Iside et Osiride,* 65: Καὶ λέγοντες θάπτεσθαι μὲν 'Οσιριν ὅτε κρύπτεται τῇ γῇ σπειρόμενος ὁ καρπός, αὖθις δ'ἀναβιοῦσθαι καὶ ἀναφαίνεσθαι ὅτε βλαστήσεως ἀρχή. See also the other texts quoted by Frazer, *op. laud.,* p. 339, n. 3.

become manifest in the crops. These spirits, keeping guard over the earth and its fruits protect them even from men themselves. When men approach to gather the harvest or reap the vintage, the most expeditious method of overcoming the spirit is to sacrifice him before the reaping. But as it is desirable to keep him in the place that he renders fruitful, the spirit of the wheat is again buried in the same soil of which he was the guardian. Usually, labourers break a statue or an image into pieces, strew over the fields the fragments, which are supposed thus to assist the process of germination.[1] In the following springtime, the god returns to life with the vegetation; every year, he thus takes upon himself again the office of guardian and undergoes his sacrifice anew.

Professor Frazer recognises in the Osirian myth all the characteristics of a worship of a spirit of vegetation.[2] Osiris would be one of those agrarian deities, who, every year, at harvest-time, are cut in pieces by the edge of the sickle or by the blows of the flail; who are buried with the seeds, and who come to birth in the springtime with the new shoots. Professor Frazer supports ably his

---

[1] For the worship of the Spirits of the corn, and for agrarian sacrifices, *cf*. Hubert and Mauss, *Essai sur le sacrifice*, p. 186.
[2] *Adonis Attis Osiris*, p. 330 *et seq.*

argument by the use of the details of the life of
Osiris given above.   Born of the sky and the earth,
as the fruitful grain is of the rain in the ground,
Osiris reveals to man the resources of agriculture;
put to death in full maturity, his dismembered
body fertilises fourteen provinces of Egypt to be
born again under the form of a tree or an ear of
corn.   I find a confirmation of this hypothesis in
several facts.   In a popular story, Isis is called
"the soul of bread" (*Bataou*); this peculiar epithet
no doubt signifies a Spirit of the corn.   Further,
Diodorus tells us that at the moment of the harvest
the Egyptian peasants wailed and besought Isis,
while they cut the first sheaf;[1] Isis, they imagined,
was mourning her husband, who died with the
dying ears of corn; and one of her tears, fallen
from the sky, made the Nile overflow and brought
about the annual inundation.[2]   Some months
later, at seedtime, the peasants buried the grain
with the same rites as those observed at the burial
of the dead.[3]   To bury the seed was indeed to bury
Osiris, the soul of the seeds; at springtime, the

[1] I, 14.
[2] According to Pausanias (in *Phocicis*, x, 32).   The Copts
have retained the Egyptian tradition and still celebrate, to-day,
on the 17th of June, the *Feast of the Fall of the Drop*, which leaving the sky brings about the inundation (J. Lieblein, ap. *Recueil
de travaux*, xxii, p. 71).
[3] *De Iside et Osiride*, 70.

new verdure gave evidence of the resurrection of the god.

As for the affinities of Osiris with the lunar god, they are in keeping with this view. It is a popular belief that the moon, to which is attributed the nightly dews, has a great influence on plant growth. "Everything grows with the growing moon, everything decreases with the waning moon," was also asserted by Pliny the Naturalist. [1] The changes in the life of the lunar Osiris correspond roughly, at any rate in the popular mind, to the alternating periods of growth and decay in the world of plants.

No doubt, the figure of Osiris is too complex for any interpretation to explain at one and the same time its diverse aspects. Nevertheless the theory that Osiris was, at least in the origin, an agrarian god, seems to me most in conformity with the spirit of the legend and the letter of the texts. If even to-day the magnificent spectacle of the death and the rebirth of the fields stirs our poetical feeling, how much more must it have impressed the fresher imaginations of our ancestors? Can we wonder that the Egyptians have incarnated in a god the annual "great affliction," and that to this god of corn and wine, who feeds men

[1] *Natural History*, ii 221. *Cf.* Frazer, *op. laud.*, p. 359 *et seq.*

with his body and blood, they have attributed the romance of a Hero and the character of a Benefactor? Osiris, in submitting himself to death, mutilation, and burial in the earth, offered himself up for the salvation of all and became a Redeemer. Resigned and confident, he revealed to mankind the way to a holy death. "Be thou faithful unto death," the Bible tells us, "and I will give thee a crown of Life." And St. Paul insists: "The body is sown in corruption . . . it is raised in glory."

It is this analogy between human destiny and vicissitudes of nature, it is the untiring hope in a springtime which shall endure for ever, that we find at the base of Egyptian thought, under the form—gradually refined to the sublime—of Osiris the Saviour.

# CHAPTER IV

## The Immortality of the Soul and Moral Retribution through the Ages

With modern people, who have attained a certain degree of culture, the idea of the immortality of the soul is closely associated with some hope of reward for a righteous life and some fear of punishment for a sinful one. If there be an existence beyond the tomb, it should be one that makes atonement for the injustices and partialities men have experienced in this earthly life; it should at the same time favour those who have lived in obedience to the dictates of their conscience. Reciprocally, the hope that there will be, after death, some retribution for the good and evil men have done on earth becomes a strong motive for belief in a future life. The immortality of the soul is one of the postulates of the idea of conscience and retribution.

Philosophers have long wondered concerning the origin of these ideas and whether they have always been in association. From the researches made into the beliefs of the peoples of classical antiquity, also of the savage tribes of our own day,[1] it has been discovered that the notion of immortality is not necessarily connected with that of retribution, nor does it appear at the same time, and the adaptation of each to the other is rather the outcome of an already advanced civilisation.

Let us make a brief inquiry of Ancient Egypt. Her monuments will allow us to go back six thousand years or more, and yield us evidence, on one side or the other, for a period covering at least four thousand years. We already know that Ancient Egypt offers particular interest in connection with this subject, because the idea of a judgment flourished there very early, and seems to have been closely connected with a traditional idea of immortality and retribution.

In order to fully understand what particular conception the Egyptians formed of immortality we must first know what they meant by the words, *life*, *death*, the *soul*.

Life, as the Egyptians imagined it, was a thing somewhat difficult to define. We moderns explain

[1] L. Marillier, *La Survivance de l'âme et l'idée de Justice chez les peuples, non civilisés (Annuaire de l'École des Hautes Études, section des Sciences religieuses,* 1894).

it as a vibration. For them, it was a breath,[1] or a fluid,[2] that could be transmitted either by sending it forth into the nostrils, or by the execution of certain magnetic passes. Daily experience showed that this breath, or motion-producing fluid, suddenly disappeared from individuals fallen into the particular condition called *death*.

This condition is characterised by the loss of consciousness, the absence of breath and movement, by the decay of the flesh and the annihilation of the body. On the other hand, this loss of consciousness, movement, and even of breath may occur frequently and temporarily in such states as sleep, a faint, or an hypnotic trance; after a variable lapse of time, the man "comes back to himself" and goes on living as before. The only serious accident of death is the decay of the body. If this can be avoided, there is no room for doubt

---

[1] "They live by breaths" in the other world (*Todtenbuch*, xxxviii, titre, xli, 2). The function of Thot, god of the wind, of the breath of life, of the Πνεῦμα, has been defined by Éd. Naville (*Zeitschrift*, 1877, p. 24). "To give the breaths" is to give life (*cf.* A. Moret, *Rituel du culte divin*, pp. 140–142). To restore a mummy, a sail was brought to his nose, to recall the breath of wind (Maspero, *Histoire*, i, p. 179). One of the ritual books which assures the resurrection of the dead is called *Book of Respirations* (*Shai n sinsin*); it has been edited and translated by J. de Horrack.

[2] *Cf.* A. Moret, *Du caractère religieux de la royauté pharaonique*, p. 45.

that breath and motion will eventually return to the dead man as they do to him who has fallen asleep or into a faint.

The Egyptians therefore explained death as an apparent and momentary suspension of life; if one understood how to exercise the arts and powers of magic, it would become possible to galvanise the bodies of people fallen into such a deplorable state to rescue them from a too protracted and dangerous interruption of life.   The essential requirement was to prevent decay, hence arose the invention of various practices, of which the best known are mummification, and of certain magic rites, called "Opening of the Mouth."[1] which were supposed to restore to the body the power of movement and the use of all its organs.   The body, being thus placed in such a condition that it can be awakened at any moment, and recalled to life, is deposited for all time in a safe tomb.   Unless some accident deteriorates the body, the life in it will never be extinguished.

There is, in fact, in the body of men, beings, and things, a permanent indestructible element, which shall survive for eternity, provided that the body, human, animal, vegetal, preserves its frame and organs uncorrupted.   We should call this

[1] A. Moret, *Rituel du culte divin*, pp. 52, 203-208.

permanent element a "corporeal soul." The
Egyptians gave it the name of *Ka* 𓂓 , that is,
"genius." Egyptologists designate it by a periphrasis: the *Double.*[1] The Double is, as it were, a
second copy of beings in their outward appearance;
it has for men the form of the human body but it is
invisible to human eyes. In order that it may
materialise itself, it must be offered a base or
support, either the living body, or the uncorrupted
corpse, or even a likeness—such as a statue, bas-
relief, or painted portrait of the living person. So,
in spite of every appearance of death in the
individual, a mummy, or portrait, provided it
possess verisimilitude, is expected to attract to it
the Double, just as the living body did, by virtue
of the fundamental principle in magic that like
attracts like.

The Double seems to have been with the Egyptians their most ancient and popular conception
of the soul. To it may be traced that first belief
in immortality which led them to build at all
times of their history those innumerable tombs
which provided for the deceased a domicile in
which the Double might enjoy eternal life. Such

[1] The theory of the Double has been explained by G. Maspero
(*Études de mythologie et d'archéologie*, i, p. 6), who has revived
a term—rather inadequate—employed by Nestor Lhôte. (*Cf.*
*Sphinx*, i, p. 67.)

8

a life is purely human and material. The man who outlives himself by his Double shall in the next world lead an existence very similar to the one he led on earth. Only, as seems natural, his life as a Double is perpetuated at the most desirable moment of his earthly existence. If he were an official, he was represented and immortalised at the height of his career, covered with glory and honour; if he were just a plain, average man, a good husband and father, his existence as a Double would afford him, eternally, all the comforts, joys, delights of an idealised home and family life. In brief, in accordance with this material conception of the soul and human idea of a future life, Paradise is little more than a well-appointed tomb, in which the Double finds a comfortable home, cool in summer, warm in winter, beautifully decorated, well stored, filled with friends, women, and flowers.

This conception lasted throughout the whole of the Egyptian civilisation and the people continued down to the Roman conquest to build for the Double these tombs, which afford us such curious realistic details about its material life after death. But, unfortunately for the believers in this matter-of-fact and comfortable future, 'a new ideal was evolving. There had been in Egypt, from the earliest known times, men who were not satisfied with this common-place destiny, this Paradise which was little more than a very desirable earth. Parallel with the belief that confines the Double to the earth, there arises a longing for the soul to leave the tomb. Out of this feeling grew another conception, probably of later date, which little by little encroached upon the primitive notion of the *Ka*, without succeeding, at any time, in completely supplanting it. It is the idea of a *spiritual* soul and of a Paradise, which in certain ways differs completely from the earthly life.

Side by side with the corporeal soul, the Egyptians imagined a soul-spirit, the *Ba*. They gave to it the shape of a bird 🐦 with a human head for it is a supernatural being, unlimited by the ordinary conditions of mankind; its intelligent head symbolises the thought that resides in the human body, while its wings are means to carry it far away from this material world. As the birds live in the sky, so the bird-soul seeks its paradise in heaven.

We do not know how the idea of a spiritual soul arose among the Egyptians. It is probable that the material life of the Double on earth seemed an unattractive and inadequate hope to the more refined and intelligent minds, nor did it suffice to overcome the fear of death. It is in the royal

pyramids of the Vth dynasty that this doctrine
of a bird-soul soaring to heaven first appears.
Among primitive peoples, however, the great of
this world carry their rank into the life beyond: the
king remains a king, the nobleman, a nobleman;
the slave, a slave. It seems probable that the
Pharaohs imagined a higher life beyond the tomb,
first for their royal persons alone. Later, by their
royal favour, their favourites and, finally, all their
subjects, were admitted to that future bliss.[1] At
any rate, under the Ancient Empire, the common
folk are satisfied with a material Paradise, where
the gods have hardly a place, receive no prayers,
and are only named that they may restore to men
a portion of the offerings[2] they have received from
them; on the other hand, the Pharaohs reserve for
themselves a more exalted abode. Their bodies
remain on earth in the Pyramids, but their souls,
knowing well all the sure ways that lead to Paradise,
edge themselves in among the gods. Some climb
thither by a ladder set up in a corner of the horizon;
some sail there in a barge wherein a suspicious
Charon plies the oars; some take a flight to the

---

[1] A. Moret, *Du caractère religieux de la royauté pharaonique*,
pp. 200-202.
[2] In the funeral formulæ of the Ancient Empire, it is said that "the
king gives the offering" to such a god "in order that he may give it"
— at least part of it—to such men as are favoured by the Pharaoh.

heavens, soaring upwards or settling on the out-spread wings of Thot, the sacred Ibis.

In heaven, the soul finds three abodes; the *Fields of Ialou*, a happy land where crops, seven cubits in height, reward the labours of the deceased; the *Fields of Offerings*, where the green meadows are spread with bread, beer and fruit, which the blessed may enjoy, without the labour of producing them; the *Solar Barge* which leads the deceased to *Douait* into the very presence of the gods themselves.[1]

Such were the diverse destinies which awaited the spiritual soul; they do not differ essentially from those offered to the corporeal soul, the Double. Each celestial paradise still savours strongly of the earth.   The Fields of Ialou are only a tract of Egyptian country transported into heaven, and the comfort enjoyed there is the comfort enjoyed by the Double in the tomb, save for the proximity of the stars and the society of the gods.   The Fields of Offerings take us a step further into the fantastical.   Here the deceased is no longer obliged to till the soil and labour for his bread.   The table is perpetually spread without effort on his part; he finds himself transported into a land of miracles. In the paradise of Douait, reached by the Solar Barge we enter into a region of marvels.   This is a

[1] See A. Moret, *In the Time of the Pharaohs*, pp. 204-205.

place of mysterious terrors as well as of celestial blisses. As the soul leaves the solid ground of the earthly paradise, it wanders farther and farther into the unknown, the uncertain, the strange, the inexplicable. In its anxious quest of its destiny beyond the tomb, the soul leads us by degrees into a new world where bliss is mingled with anxiety.

Therefore, we are not surprised when we find that as far back as this time the aspirations for immortality are tinged with scepticism. As early as the XIth dynasty there was chanted on the day of the funeral, a dirge that to us sounds pessimistic. "Tears cannot bring back to life the heart of him who goes down to the tomb. Therefore make ye a holiday while ye are on the earth and be ye not weary of the holiday. It is not granted to any to take his goods into the other world and there is none who went there who has returned hither." Did the yearning for a paradise, farther and farther away, more mysterious, hence less certain, make men fear whether they would ever attain it and enjoy any paradise at all? Be that as it may, the more we advance in Egyptian history, the stronger grows the spirit of scepticism.[1]

[1] See *The Songs of the Harpist* engraved in the Theban tombs of the New Empire and reproduced in *In the Time of the Pharaohs,* pp. 264-265.

The faith in immortality, so firmly rooted in the minds of the early Egyptians, begins to waver as soon as man tries to reason and therefore to doubt.

Along with reason, another anxiety arose, a moral qualm as to what will befall man in the other world; what, there, awaits his good or evil deeds. This idea of retribution is expressed in a popular tradition, narrated by Diodorus[1] when writing concerning the judgment of the dead in Egypt.

Moreover, the friends and nearest relations of the dead acquaint the judges and the rest of their friends with the time prefixed for the funeral of such an one by name, declaring that such a day he is to pass the Lake. At which time forty-two judges appear and sit together in a semicircle, in a place beyond the Lake, where a ship provided beforehand by those who have charge of the matter and directed by a pilot whom the Egyptians call Charon is hauled up to the shore.[2] . . . The ship, being now in the Lake, every one is at liberty by the law to accuse the dead before the coffin be put aboard; and if any accuser appear and make good his accusation, that he lived an ill life, then the judges give sentence, and the body is debarred from being buried after the usual manner; but if the informer be

[1] *Diodorus*, i, 7. Trans.: G. Booth.

[2] According to the Egyptian texts, the divine ferryman was called Mahaf; but the word *qaro* means *boat* in Egyptian. Concerning the character of the boat which conveyed the dead to heaven or to the tomb, *cf.* Lefébure, *La Barque*, ap. *Sphinx* vii, p. 185 *et seq.*

convicted of a scandalous and malicious accusation, he is very severely punished.   If no informer appear, or if the information prove false, all the kindred of the deceased leave off mourning and begin to set forth his praises. . . .   The common people take up the strain and approve of all that is said in his praise with a loud shout, and set forth likewise his virtues with the highest praises and strains of commendation as he that is to live for ever in the kingdom of the other world.

In reality, this tribunal of justice was supposed by the Egyptians, to sit, not on earth but in the other world, and the living had no part in the judgment.   In the realm of the dead, there was said to be a Hall of the Double Justice, where the deceased was tried before a jury consisting of forty-two divinities and one supreme judge, Osiris.[1]   The attention of all was concentrated upon a divine balance by which stood the god Thot, superintending the weighing.   In one scale lay the heart of the deceased, that is, his conscience heavy with sin or light.   In the other scale was truth, symbolised by a statuette of the goddess Maît, or by a feather ʃ, a hieroglyphic of the goddess.   When the weight of the heart equalled the weight of the truth, then the account given by the deceased of his conduct on earth was held

[1] *In the Time of the Pharaohs*, p. 234 *et seq.*

to be proved true. Thot and Osiris verified with a plumb line the accuracy of the balance, and if it was satisfactory, admitted the deceased to Paradise. In a case to the contrary the deceased was sentenced to infernal tortures. Such, in broad outline, is the judgment of the dead. I have shown elsewhere[1] how the tribunal of Osiris, at its inception influenced by bribery, threats, and trickery, developed an increasing sense of impartiality and integrity. In its highest form, it shows us divine justice, no longer satisfied with merely inquiring into the deeds of the deceased, but careful to secure for those who have suffered unjustly from men or fate during their life on earth, a reward proportionate to their deserts and to their sufferings.

Through the whole course of its evolution, the judgment of the dead in Egypt retains three important features: *first*, a tribunal, consisting of a supreme judge, Osiris, god of the Nether World; assisted by the goddesses of Truth (the double Mait), certain psychopomps (leaders of the soul) such as Anubis, Thot, and forty-two assessors, who perform the office of an examining jury; *second*, a balance with two scales; *third*, an executioner, who, under the form of a hybrid monster,

[1] *In the Time of the Pharaohs*, p. 241 *et seq.*

watches the weighing, ready to devour the soul that is found wanting. This method of judgment by weighing the souls—or *psychostasy*—can be traced back to at least 2000 B.C.[1]

The idea that divine justice can become materialised in a balance and human deeds be estimated by their weight is common to other nations of antiquity. Psychostasy of the same kind appears in their religious texts upon their monuments, and it has kept a prominent place in the Christian iconography down to the Middle Ages. Let us see, then, how the Greeks, Romans, Persians, Hindoos, Jews, Christians, and Mohammedans embodied this idea of which we have found so clear an expression in Egypt.

In Greece, the weighing of the deeds of men occurs in the Homeric Poems. In the *Iliad*, when Zeus desired to decide upon the issue of a conflict between two armies or two warriors,

then did the Father balance his golden scales, and put therein two fates of death (χῆρε) that bringeth long woe, one for horse-taming Trojans, one for mail-clad Achaians; and he took the scale-yard by the

[1] The principle of the Judgment of the Dead by the Balance was admitted from the time of the Pyramids of the VIth dynasty (see *In the Time of the Pharaohs*, p. 214); but representations of the Judgment are not known before the time of the New Empire, about 1600 B.C.

midst and lifted it, and the Achaians' day of destiny sank. So lay the Achaians' fates on the bounteous earth, and the Trojans' fates were lifted up towards wide heaven.[1]

The same operation is described, in the same terms, at the moment when Achilles and Hector meet in single combat.[2] These passages have been imitated literally by Virgil in the description of the struggle between Æneas and Turnus:

Jupiter himself holds forth two scales with balance poised, and in them puts the opposite fortunes (*fata*) of the two, to discover which of them the sinking scale is to doom, with the weight of which death is to incline.[3]

As De Witte, who first compared these texts, has well put it,[4]

in Homer, there is nothing to suggest that psychostasy is concerned with a future life and the rewards and punishments which await man there. . . . It is only the question of the issue of a contest. . . . The weighing of the fates or souls has no other aim than the decision of an earthly and material conflict. It is the lightest weight that indicates the victor.

The Homeric psychostasy in the *Iliad* has nothing to do with divine justice; it is a weighing

---

[1] *Iliad.*, viii.   Trans.: Lang, Leaf, and Myers, p. 145.
[2] *Ibid.*, p. 440.                    [3] *Æneid*, xii, 725-727.
[4] De Witte, *Scènes de la Psychostasie homérique*, ap. *Revue archéologique*, January 15, 1845, p. 647.

of destinies. We learn from Plutarch that at a very early date, as far back as the time of Æschylus, the weighing of the destinies of Achilles and Hector went by the name of ψυχοστασία, "psychostasy"— the weighing of souls.[1] This scene is frequently represented on painted vases where the fates or souls assume the form of little fighting warriors or of little naked winged genii.[2] Here, fate has already taken an individual character; in estimating its weight the moral value of the individual must henceforth be taken into account.

In fact, we learn from the *Odyssey* that the idea of a tribunal which sat in Hades to judge the dead was already familiar to the Greeks. It is said of Minos, the ancient King of Crete, that he ruled in the Infernal Regions and that, assisted by his brothers Æacus and Rhadamanthus, he presided over this tribunal.[3]  "There then I saw Minos,

---

[1] De Witte, *loc. cit.*, p. 653.  Æschylus, by what Plutarch says, founded upon this episode in the legend of Hector and Achilles, a tragedy, entitled *Psychostasia*.

[2] See an Etruscan mirror, in the *Recherches sur la Psychostasie* (ap. *Revue archéologique*, August 15, 1844, p. 297), published by Maury.  The Stadtholders' Vase and the Vase from the Luynes collection (*ap.* De Witte, *loc. cit.*, pp. 650 and 652).

[3] *Odyssey*, iv, 564.  The Greek name Rhadamanthus calls up the memory of the Egyptian word *Amenti*, "the west, the other world," and of the epithet "chief of the Amenti," which is that of the Egyptian funeral gods.  *Cf.* V. Bérard, *Les Phéniciens et l'Odyssée*, ii, p. 69.

glorious son of Zeus, wielding a golden sceptre,
giving sentence from his throne to the dead, while
they sat and stood around the prince, asking his
dooms through the wide-gated house of Hades."[1]
This refers unmistakably to a tribunal of the dead,
but there is not the least suggestion that judgment
is being passed upon deeds performed by the dead
while they were alive upon the earth.  It is just
possible that Minos, Æacus, and Rhadamanthus
simply continue to exercise in Hades the office of
judge which is an essential prerogative of primitive
kingship.[2]  The cases brought before them may be
conflicts that have arisen in the Nether World,
for there "is strife among men" in Hades as well as
on earth.  Nowhere in the *Odyssey* do we find,
clearly expressed, the idea that men shall have to
account for their earthly deeds before the tribunal
of Minos.

The first mention of it in Greek literature is in
Pindar, at the beginning of the fifth century.  In
the second *Olympic*, the poet says, "The great of
the Earth shall find a judge in Hades, for they
atone by sufferings (ποινὰς ἔτισαν); those who on

---

[1] *Odyssey*, xi, 567–570.
[2] For all the classical texts and their commentaries, I refer,
henceforward, to the excellent monograph of Ruhl, *De mortuorum
judicio*, Giessen, 1903.

Earth have committed evil deeds are judged by the goddess Ananke."[1]

This statement marks a great advance in the idea of justice; the tribunal in Hades prosecutes for sins committed on earth, but what system of procedure was followed by Ananke or the divine tribunal, we do not learn. It is from Plato that we derive further information.

In the *Apology of Socrates*, the poet-philosopher sets over against human tribunals, or rather "those who pretend to be judges . . . those who are true judges, and who are said to judge in the infernal regions, Minos, Rhadamanthus, Æacus, and Triptolemus, and such other of the demi-gods as were righteous during their own life." We see at once that such a court constitutes itself the guardian of virtue and will therefore demand that men should justify their earthly actions. In the *Gorgias*, Plato develops this idea very elaborately:

This law respecting men was in existence in the time of Saturn, and always was and still is, established

[1] *Olympic*, ii, 56 *et seq.*

> τάδ' ἐν τᾷδε Διὸς ἀρχᾷ
> ἀλιτρὰ κατὰ γᾶς δικάζει τις ἐχθρὰ
> λόγον φράσαισ' Ἀνάγκα

*Cf.* Ruhl, p. 34 *et seq.*

among the gods, that *a man who has passed through life justly and piously* should when he dies go to the *Islands of the Blessed*, and dwell in all perfect happiness free from evil, but that he who has lived *unjustly and impiously* should go to a prison of punishment and justice, which they call *Tartarus*.

During the reign of Saturn, and even recently when Jupiter held the government, there were *living judges of the living*, who passed sentence on the very day on which any one was about to die. In consequence of this, sentences were badly awarded.    Pluto, therefore, and the guardians of the Blessed Isles, went to Jupiter and informed him that men came to them who did not deserve either sentence.

Jupiter, therefore, said, I will prevent this in future. For now sentences are badly awarded, because those that are judged are judged clothed, for they are judged while living.    Many, therefore, he continued, whose souls are depraved are invested with beautiful bodies, nobility of birth, and riches, and when the judgment takes place, many witnesses come in their behalf, to testify that they have lived justly.    Hence the judges are awed by these things, and moreover, they too pass sentence when clothed, for their minds are veiled with eyes and ears, and the whole body. . . .    Therefore . . . they must be judged divested of all these things; for they must be judged after they are dead; the judge too must be naked and dead . . . destitute of all his kindred, and leaving all that ornament on the earth in order that the judgment may be just.

"Now I had observed these things . . . and accordingly have appointed my sons as judges, two from Asia, Minos and Rhadamanthus, and one from Europe, Æacus. These, then, when they are dead, shall judge in the meadow, at the three roads, of which two lead, one to the Isles of the Blessed, the other to Tartarus. And Rhadamanthus shall judge those from Asia, and Æacus those from Europe. But to Minos I will give the prerogative of deciding in case any doubt occurs to the two others. . . .

". . . When, therefore, they come to the judge . . . Rhadamanthus, having made them stand before him, examines the soul of each, not knowing whose it is. . . ." If this soul is filled with disorder and baseness, having lived far from the truth, Rhadamanthus "sends it ignominiously to prison, where on its arrival it will undergo the punishment it deserves." Those who can expiate their offences, do so by sufferings. But those who have committed the greatest sins are incurable. Punishment is useless to them, but it serves as an example to others. Rhadamanthus "sends them to Tartarus, signifying at the same time whether they appear to be curable or incurable, but arriving thither, they suffer according to their deserts.

Sometimes, Rhadamanthus beholding another soul that has passed through life piously and with truth, . . . is delighted, and sends it to the Isles of the Blessed."[1] Æacus, too, does the same and, like Minos, he gives his verdict with a whip in his hand.

[1] *Gorgias.* Trans.: Cary, p. 228 *et seq.*

By the fourth century B.C., the divine tribunal
has thus become an elaborate organisation.  The
judges are the three traditional kings who date
back to Homeric times; but instead of discharging
the duties of their office as a kingly prerogative
divorced from ethics, they endeavour to appreciate
at their just value the vices and virtues of
humanity and to assign to men different abodes
according to their works.  The truly righteous
enjoy the Islands of the Blessed; the unrepentant
wicked endure torments in Tartarus; while the
neutrals serve a term of probation in a kind of
purgatory, in order to atone for their misdeeds.

It is to be remarked that Pindar and Plato, who
formulated—the former in a few words, the latter
in many pages—the theory of a judgment in the
other world, probably derived their inspiration
from the Orphic and the Pythagorean doctrines.[1]

On the other hand, the tragic poets and orators
make but brief allusions to the subject of judgment,
nor is the store of funeral inscriptions that have
come down to us of any use; far from supplying
any information on how the common folk imagined
judgment, they leave the point untouched.  Are

---

[1] This point was made clear by A. Dietrich and after him by
L. Ruhl from fragments of Orphic writings and scenes on painted
vases.   L. Ruhl, *De mortuorum judicio*, p. 46 *et seq.*

we to infer from this silence that the theory of a judgment of the dead never went beyond the limits of philosophical and poetical speculation?[1]

Little wonder, then, if the matter-of-fact, and practical-minded Stoics and Epicureans dismissed the fable of judgment with a contempt, imitated later by certain Latin writers, notably Cicero and Seneca.[2]  The Latin poets, however, mention the infernal judges—Horace in his *Odes*,[3] then Ovid,[4] and especially Virgil.  The sixth book of the *Æneid* reveals how the Latin mind, during the first century of our era, imitated and developed the theme.

When Æneas descends into Hades, he notices that the dead are sent either to Tartarus or to the Elysian Fields.  "And these abodes are by no means assigned without allotment, without a judge; Minos rules the scrutiny and shakes the urn, he convokes the silent dead and learns their lives and the charges brought against them."[5] The poet further describes his wanderings in the Nether World; the way divides into two paths, the right leads to Elysium, but, by the left, the

---

[1] L. Ruhl, *De mortuorum judicio*, pp. 67–74.

[2] *Ibid.*, pp. 54, 75

[3] II, 13, 22; iv, 7, 21.

[4] XIII, 25.                [5] *Æneid*, vi, 426 *et seq.*

dead arrive at Tartarus where they receive their punishment. Here Rhadamanthus is lord and rules with stern severity.[1]

The other poets, from Propertius to Seneca and from Statius to Claudianus, take up the topic treated by Virgil, impressing upon it a strongly Latin character. With them, the tribunal of the dead takes on the semblance of a Roman tribunal as already pointed out by Servius in his commentary upon the *Æneid;* Minos is a Roman quæstor, who draws lots to determine in what order the cases shall be examined; Rhadamanthus strikes the criminals with his sceptre, while the Furies lash with their whips those who will not confess their crimes. Vivid and impressive as is this description, it remains none the less a purely literary exercise. The unlearned knew little about the judgment of the dead, and the cultivated few made a jest of it as a poetical invention.

This is evidenced by the presentment of divine justice in the famous *Dialogues of the Dead* by Lucian of Samosata about 170 A.D. A certain highwayman, Sostrates, is sentenced by Minos to everlasting torments. But he disputes the verdict, questions the authority of the judges, arguing, upon the assumption that all the events of his

[1] *Æneid*, vi, 566 *et seq.*

life were prearranged by the Fates and by Destiny, and therefore he cannot be held responsible for his doings. Minos, overcome by the truth of the logical deduction, releases the culprit, but with these warning words: "Mind that thou dost not teach the dead to argue as thou hast done." In the form of a jest, this criticism dismisses the belief in a judgment of human actions among men who submit their lives to Ananke and Fatum. The paradoxical result is that in the last centuries of the Græco-Roman civilisation, the sceptical dilettanti speak, without any faith in it, of a judgment of the dead, and in the very terms used in times long past by the Homeric bards; both subordinating divine equity to inevitable fate.

If we now turn to the Eastern civilisations, we find that the tradition of a judgment of the dead is presented in a different way in the Avesta, the Vedas, and in some of the Buddhic hymns.

The Avesta, the holy book of Persia, is not known in its original form; the texts we possess were collected in the third century A.D., under the dynasty of the Sassanides. They afford us an entirely new conception of the judgment.

After man has gone, is dead, the impious and malevolent spirits begin their attacks. After the third

night, at dawn, when day is breaking, Mithra, well-
armed, comes to the mountain and the sun rises.
Then the demon . . . carries away in chains the
sinful souls of wicked mortals. The soul follows the
road built by Time, a road built for the wicked as well
as for the righteous, the bridge *Cinvat* constructed by
Mazda. Arrived there, the conscience (the soul
*dæna*) . . . drags down the souls of the wicked into
the darkness, but bears up the souls of the faithful
over the bridge *Cinvat*, into the way of the gods.[1]

Here a distinction is drawn between virtue and
sin; the wicked are punished, while the righteous
are rewarded. But a new element is introduced,
the test of the *bridge*, which the righteous alone
may cross in safety, an allegory that we shall find
elsewhere and which takes us away from the traditional *weighing of the soul*.

The *weighing of the soul* before a tribunal,
appears, however, in the later texts interpolated
into the Avesta by the Pehlevi theologians.

The chief judge is Mithra, the god of the Sun, of
Truth and of Justice. Near him, Rashnu holds a
*golden balance* in the scales of which the deeds of
men are placed. "He does not cause the divine
balance to drop one way or the other,[2] either for

---

[1] Söderblom, *La vie future d'après le Mazdéisme*, p. 85 (Musée
Guimet, *Bibliothèque d' études*, t. ix).

[2] This phrase often appears also in the Egyptian texts for the
estimating of human or divine justice.

the good or for the wicked, either for kings or for emperors; he doth not cause it to stir a hair's breadth, and he shows no favour." A scrupulous regard for justice is revealed in another feature. Men whose good and evil deeds are of equal weight are sent to a *purgatory* (Hamestagan), an intermediate stage between hell and the abode of the good.

Finally, the still later texts of the Avesta present a judgment of a new type, *the last judgment*, which shall take place at the end of the world. According to a very ancient tradition, the earth shall perish in a great fire. There shall come a time when a supreme judge, Soshyans, shall begin his reign. Then shall begin the resurrection of the dead, and it shall be complete in fifty-seven years. All the world shall be gathered together in one large assembly and each man shall come face to face with his good or evil deeds. The pious man shall go at once to Paradise, but the impious shall spend three days and three nights of torment in hell. Then a meteor falling from the moon, shall set the earth on fire. And from the fire men shall arise purified, and begin on earth a new life eternal, in which there shall be no stain of evil and therefore no second judgment. It will be remarked how in this eschatological conception, the scruples of conscience have made the tradition of a cosmic cataclysm, which shall bring about the end of the world, serve an ethical purpose, although, originally, this final cataclysm had nothing to do with ethics.

In India, the *Rig-Veda*, which dates at least as far back as the tenth century B.C., does not give a very clear account of any judgment of the dead. Two gods, however, play an active part towards the deceased.    One is Yama, the first of the living, who, like Osiris in Egypt, knew death and having become a god of the dead, seems to point out to mankind the way to the world beyond.    He is aided in his task by messengers, who, under the guise of dogs (here, again, we recall the Egyptian Anubis), go in search of men, guide them, and act as psychopomp deities.    The other god is Varouna, the lord of vengeance and penalties, who controls the deeds of the dead.    The righteous are allowed to live in the light near Yama and Varouna, while the impious and unrighteous, those who have sinned against the gods, must discharge the debts they have incurred, and it is to Varouna they must render their account.    There is, here, no question of a tribunal, or of a last judgment, only of a limited divine justice dealing with crimes committed against the gods. So was it in the first ages of the Egyptian civilisation; the gods did not concern themselves with the conduct of man towards man; they inquired only whether he had discharged his duty towards the gods themselves.

In the Buddhist books, the writing of which was begun in the fifth century B.C., a higher ideal appears. Buddha showed men the way to redemption. In order to attain true life, every being must pass through a cycle of existences, each more sanctified than the last, by the renunciation of worldly joys, the annulment of all desires. According to this new conception, death does not confer a new life upon the righteous. On the contrary, perfect living ends in the annihilation of conscious and responsible existence in the abyss of Nirvana. A sort of automatic justice is meted out, not to the part we call the human soul, but to the *karman*, the permanent element in every being that ensures the continuity of the individual through his successive lives. There is no need of a judgment giving access to Paradise or Hell; for immanent justice determines after man's successive deaths, the condition of his future existences or his final deliverance.

At a later period when Buddhism was adopted in other countries where the idea of judgment was either traditional or an outgrowth of the Mazdean and Hellenic doctrines it has been recently discovered how strong their influence was in other fields, like those of the plastic arts and dramatic poetry—we see that the notions of a weighing of the soul, judgment of the dead, Paradise and Hell, impressed themselves upon Buddhist art and theology. In a Buddhist picture described by Maury, the dwellings of the gods are represented with earth and hell beneath them. In the upper part of hell, Yama is seated on a throne; in his right hand he holds a kind of fork, in his left, a mirror in which are reflected the good and evil deeds of those called up for judgment. On the left of Yama stands a personage who holds a balance by the middle of its beam and weighs the bodies of the deceased. At the foot of Yama's throne, "are two spirits, one good, the other evil; they shake sacks full of pebbles which represent the good and evil deeds of men—the pebbles of the former white, of the latter black. Beneath are portrayed the torments of hell."[1] Owing to its universal and profoundly human character, the idea of judgment and psychostasy found its way everywhere. It could be reconciled with doc-

---

[1] *Revue archéologique*, 1844, p. 294.

trines fundamentally opposed, like metempsycho-
sis and Nirvana.

If, now, we turn from Oriental mythology to
Christianity, we are again met by the belief in a
last judgment which shall call men together at the
end of time. But the conception is different from
that propounded in the sacred books of Iran. The
Avesta states that the world will end in a great
cataclysm of nature, by fire, and that the last
judgment shall take place simultaneously. But
the catastrophe is not presented as a consequence
of the misdeeds of the sons of men. With the
Semites, on the contrary, the idea of the last
judgment is rooted in a purely metaphysical and
ethical doctrine. The Lord will purge the earth
from evil by a definitive judgment, which shall
be like the deluge, a manifestation of divine justice
finally victorious over the sin and wickedness of
the world.

The gospel according to St. Matthew[1] describes
the Last Judgment in the following terms:

When the Son of man shall come in his glory, and all
the holy angels with him, then shall he sit upon the
throne of his glory; and before him shall be gathered
all nations; and he shall separate them one from

[1] Chap. xxv.

another, as a shepherd divideth his sheep from the goats; and he shall set the sheep on his right hand, but the goats on the left.  Then shall the King say unto them on his right hand, Come, ye blessed of my Father, inherit the kingdom prepared for you from the foundation of the world; for I was an hungered, and ye gave me meat; I was thirsty, and ye gave me drink; I was a stranger, and ye took me in; naked, and ye clothed me. . . .  Then shall he say also unto them on the left hand, Depart from me, ye cursed, into everlasting fire.

It is easy to trace in this account the essential features of the Egyptian tradition.  Amon-Râ, the divine judge, also places the righteous on his right and sends the wicked to hell-fire.  Christ's words of commendation regarding the good deeds of the righteous are identical with those pronounced by the Egyptian deceased when he comes before the tribunal of Osiris and enumerates the merits of his life on earth.  "I live by the truth, I have propitiated God by my love; I have given bread to the hungry, water to the thirsty, and garments to the naked."

Also in the Apocalypse, which so often reveals the impress of Oriental tradition, we should note

[1] *Cf.* A. Moret, *In the Time of the Pharaohs*, p. 258 *et seq.*  Let it be added that upon a stela of the XIIth dynasty, Osiris already places the just "on his right" (Louvre, Stèle C, 3, l. 19).

the apparition of an angel mounted on a black horse, holding a balance in his hands.[1]

We may note, further, the following features:

And I saw the dead, small and great, stand before God; and the books were opened . . . and the dead were judged out of those things which were written in the books, according to their works. . . . This is the second death. And whosoever was not found written in the book of life was cast into the lake of fire.[2]

The same idea of a second death of the wicked in hell is fully expressed in the Egyptian *Book of the Dead;* even the texts of the Pyramids of the Vth dynasty already point out that the dead must be judged according to their deeds and their names inscribed in the Book of Life in the next world, if they are to enjoy a second life there.[3]

Christianity has preserved side by side the two forms of judgment; individual, at the death of each man; the final, or last judgment, at the end of the world. This twofold theme was treated by the artists who decorated our cathedrals, and by the author-monks, who wrote thereon many an edifying treatise. "Psychostasy generally forms

[1] Revelation, vi, 5.    *Cf.* Maury, *Revue archéologique,* 1844, p. 300.

[2] Revelation, xx, 12–15.

[3] A. Moret, *In the Time of the Pharaohs,* p. 211.

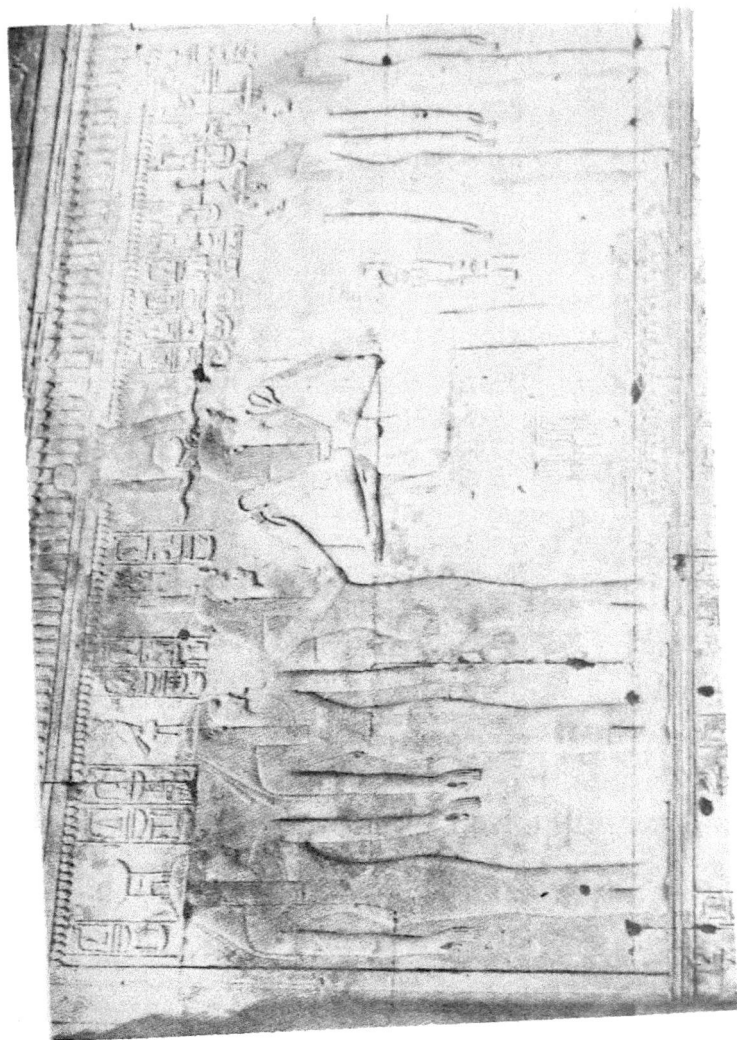

Osiris Adored by Justice (Truth). (Maāt).

(Abydos, temple de Seti I).

a subject which is treated apart and is frequently
represented on the capitals of the pillars in our
churches.[1] . . . The same scenes are seen in the
miniature paintings in manuscripts from the thir-
teenth century to the sixteenth."[2] Sometimes
the psychostasy is but one episode in the great
scene of the Last Judgment or of the Resurrection;
it is then God Himself or the Archangel Michael
who holds the scales. But in the Lives of the
Saints, the weighing of the soul is not generally
associated with the Last Judgment. Like the
Egyptians and the Greek disciples of Plato, the
Christians of the Middle Ages believed that
the test of the divine balance would be applied to
each man individually as soon as he had drawn his
last breath. The word of the Bible, "Thou hast
been weighed in the balance and found wanting,"
was read not in the spirit but in the letter, as is
proved by many a story in the Golden Legend.
As recently as the eighteenth century, a preacher
spoke of the individual judgment as of a case
coming before the tribunal of God; the accused,
assailed by demons, defended by the Virgin

[1] The church of the Holy Cross in St.-Lô; the church of Monte-
villiers, the church of Saint-Nectaire, and on bas-reliefs in Saint-
Trophime in Arles.

[2] Maury, *Revue archéologique*, 1844, p. 236. *Cf.* E. Mâle,
*L'art religieux du XIIIe siècle, en France*, p. 476 *et seq.*

and the Saints, was undergoing trial for many days.[1]

It was natural that the doctrine of Mahomet should retain many features of the Eastern tradition. Take, for example, this description of the Last Judgment from the Koran.

When therefore the trumpet shall be sounded, there shall be no relation between them which shall be regarded on that day; neither shall they ask assistance of each other. They whose balances shall be heavy with good works, shall be happy; but they whose balances shall be light, are those who shall lose their souls, and shall remain in hell for ever.[2]

Besides the weighing of the soul, the Koran presents another allegory of judgment, the Mazdean test of the bridge, which was crossed easily by the righteous, but which proves a pitfall to the wicked.

[1] See the facts quoted by Maury, *Revue archéologique*, 1844, pp. 236–249. Paulin Paris (*Catalogue des manuscrits français*, t. iv, p. 4) has published the case "of a clerk who was weighed in the balance by Mgr. Saint-Michel, upon the accusation of an enemy." The soul was placed in the balance before God together "with all the good he had said or done in his life, and on the other side the evil that the enemy brought." And it was found that the evil weighed marvellously more than the good. But the Virgin Mary made the terrible balance weigh down on the other side, by putting into the good scale all the *Ave-Marias* that the clerk had recited." In Egypt, the heart must not weigh heavier than the truth.

[2] Koran, xxiii, 7.

The bridge (called in Arabic *al Sirat*), which they say is laid over the midst of hell, is described to be "finer than a hair, and sharper than the edge of a sword; . . . the good shall pass with wonderful ease and swiftness like lightning or the wind; whereas the wicked . . . fall down headlong into hell, which is gaping beneath them."[1]

It is curious to see how this tradition impressed Christian belief.   As proof, instance the story in the dialogues of St. Gregory the Great.[2]"

A soldier died of the plague in Constantinople.   By the grace of God, his soul returned to his body, so that he was able to relate his experiences in the other world.   He told there was a bridge, beneath which flowed a river and its waters were black. . . . Beyond the bridge stretched green and smiling meadows, enamelled with sweet-smelling flowers, and therein walked men clad in white apparel, breathing forth a fragrant perfume.   And upon the bridge men underwent a test.   When the wicked tried to cross it, they fell into the dark and putrid river; whereas the righteous passed safely over, and entered into security in the pleasant pastures.

Thus there are transmitted from religion to religion, the most diverse traditions concerning the judgment.

[1] Koran, Preliminary Discourse, Sale, p. 71.
[2] Maury, *loc. cit*, p. 297.

To sum up, a belief in a judgment of souls and the material instruments to secure it—such as the balance—are common to many peoples of antiquity. In the earliest historical times, justice is rudimentary. Be it Osiris, Minos, Yama, or Varouna, who presides over the tribunal, they all judge men on utilitarian principles, not according to what Kant has termed the categorical imperative. As human conscience develops, God, or the gods, are represented more perfect, and they in théir turn require greater perfection from their subjects. Divine Justice is made guardian of the law and of ethics. It demands retribution and redresses wrong. This stage once reached, men no longer discriminate between Justice and God, and lofty speculations arise upon the metaphysical nature of Justice and Truth.

In the Avesta, for instance, Justice becomes a divinity that any man creates by his own good deeds, and who takes on the shape of a fair maiden who welcomes the righteous into another world.

At the end of the third night, as day is breaking, the soul of the righteous man wanders forth into a land of flowers and perfumes. A wind, more fragrant than any wind that blows, comes to him from the south. . . . Wafted upon this breeze, the faithful soul sees his religion (or conscience, *daêna*)˙coming to meet him under the guise of a young maiden, beautiful, shining, lusty, her arms white, her limbs rounded, her breasts firm and curved, a goodly frame with the grace of her fifteen years, and as fair in form as the fairest creature that breathes. . . . Then the soul of the faithful asks: "What virgin art thou, loveliest to gaze upon of all the virgins I have ever seen?" . And she replies to him: "O young man of noble mind, of good works, of good actions, of good religion, I am thine own embodied conscience . . . thou didst love me for my majesty, my beauty.   Lovable, thou hast made me more lovable; fair, thou hast made me fairer; desirable, thou hast made me more desirable. . . . Go forth into the Eternal Light.[1]

In the Vedas, the intimate union of Beauty and Righteousness is no less forcibly expressed.   Good and Evil are none other than Truth and Falsehood. God is Truth and lives by Truth.

Plato comes to the same conclusion when he describes the abode of the gods and tries to give a definition of divine thought.   The immortals live in an ideal region, the Fields of Truth.

Real existence, colourless, formless, and intangible, visible only to the intelligence which sits at the helm of the soul, and with which the family of true science is concerned, has its abode in this region.   The mind of deity, as it is fed by intelligence and pure science and the mind of every soul that is destined to receive its

---

[1] Söderblom, *loc. cit.*, p. 83.   *Cf.* Lefébure, ap. *Sphinx*, viii, p. 39.

due inheritance, is raptured at seeing the essence to which it has so long been a stranger, and by the light of truth is fostered and made to thrive. . . . It sees distinctly absolute justice, absolute temperance, and absolute science; the justice, the temperance, the science which exist in that which is real and essential being. . . . Such is the life of the gods.[1]

Many centuries earlier the Egyptians had held a similar doctrine. The hymns sung to the gods about the XIXth dynasty, 1200 years B.C., prove that at this time the cultivated minds did not discriminate between Truth-Justice and the Supreme Intelligence. What lies behind appearances, what really exists, is Truth and Justice. To do what is true is to do as the gods do, is to become a God.[2] Thus men cast off their mortal nature and passing into another world put on in its place, a divine one. The Bible word, "I am the Truth and the Life," expresses perfectly the highest conception of divinity formed by the Egyptians. Of the many methods offered to the Egyptians whereby they could secure in the next world the favour of God, the one most likely to attract the greater number of people was undoubtedly magic. But the minds, with noble aspirations cherished a higher ideal "to offer to God a sacrifice of Justice," "to practise

[1] Phædrus. Trans.: Wright, pp. 49–50.
[2] *In the Time of the Pharaohs*, p. 256 *et seq.*

truth which God loves, " [1] and so, instead of striving to overcome God by violence or to outwit him by magic tricks, they sought to become like unto him and thus to attain unto divinity.

[1] Texts of the VIth dynasty.

# CHAPTER V

## THE MYSTERIES OF ISIS

ABOUT the beginning of the Christian era,
Egypt, for the past three centuries under the
rule of the Greeks, was conquered by Octavius
and became the personal property of the Roman
Emperors. Reduced, thus, to a state of servitude,
her national life dwindled away; Christianity
was the last factor in the transformation and
gave the final blow to the decaying language,
customs, and gods of Egypt. But, at the very
moment when the Egyptian religion was dying
in its native land, it underwent a new birth in a
region where it was little expected, in Italy and the
Western Roman Empire. Osiris and Isis, the most
popular of the gods once worshipped on the banks
of the Nile, emigrated into the Roman world
converted to their doctrines.

In the days when the Ptolemies controlled the
whole Mediterranean, their State gods, Serapis
and Isis, set out from Alexandria along with the

Egyptian missionaries and landed at Cyprus, Antioch, Delos, and Sicily, where temples were raised to them. They crossed the sea, yet again, in trading-vessels, and their cult was spread abroad by the merchants and sailors, who all worshipped Isis, star of the sea, protector of seafaring men. Leaving the ports of the Hellenic Mediterranean, their galleys sailed along the coast of Italy, Gaul, and Spain, bringing the worship of Isis to all the places they visited, and leaving everywhere behind them testimony, precious to us, in the form of statuettes recently discovered, which have revealed how widespread was the cult of the Egyptian goddess.

Throughout Pharaonic Egypt, Isis held a position subordinate to Osiris. But when Herodotus visited Egypt, she was already on the way to become the most popular divinity,[1] universally beloved and worshipped. Osiris, the god who had taught men how to overcome the fear of death, owed his miraculous resurrection to the love and magic knowledge of his wife.[2] Looking closely into the matter, was it not rather Isis who rescued gods and men from death? With the feeling of gratitude towards her as a saviour-goddess was blended the special attraction, to be found in all

[1] *Herodotus*, ii, 100.     [2] *De Iside et Osiride*, 27.

religions, exercised by a deity who symbolises and sublimates in herself the ideal of wifehood and motherhood. For these reasons, the devotees, who in the first centuries of our era received the Osirian doctrines, adopted the patronage of the god dess rather than of the god,[1] becoming known, in the Roman world, by the name of Isiacs and soon dominating all other sects in the Empire.

How can this wonderful vogue be explained? In Greece, as in Italy, the State religion had failed to provide men with a lofty ideal and an ethical standard of life. Vulgar superstition, rites either barbarous or become meaningless, puerile or immoral legends—such were the externals of a religion that had long ago lost its vitality and had become, as Lucretius puts it, "the cause of so much evil." The priest left to the philosophers investigations concerning the immortality of the soul, divine justice, the hope of an eternal life and retribution. But the speculations of a Pythagoras, the sublime meditations of a Plato, were known only to a few. Not far from Greece, in that mysterious land of Egypt, there had lived men, "the most religious of men," according to Herod-

[1] In the Roman epoch, many of the women initiated into the Osirian rites were no longer called "Osiris Such-an-one" but "Hathorian Such-an-one," which indicates the prevalence of the worship of Isis–Hathor.

otus, faithful, for thousands of years to the same
gods. These gods had called the whole nation,
high and low, to salvation, had taught men how to
live in wisdom in order to be reborn divine after
death. These revelations, the possession of all
Egyptians, penetrated into Greece in the guise
of secret doctrines—the Orphic rites and the
Eleusinian mysteries.[1]  Though we know that in
either one the speculations concerning the future
life and the means whereby to obtain it are derived
from an Egyptian source, we must not consider
them as servile imitators of Egyptian beliefs.
Both doctrines seem to have been strongly influenced by Egypt but to have developed on Greek
lines. It is only after the Ptolemies established
their rule in Egypt that the Greek world became
open to Alexandrine philosophy and Alexandrine
gods. It was only after Egypt had become the
crown property of the Cæsars that the Roman
world began to be invaded by the statues of Osiris
and Isis, accompanied by their priests.

The Isiac propaganda enlisted not only the
humble and poor, to whom it held out consolatory
hopes of future happiness, but, also, the cultivated
upper classes,—philosophers, artists, and men of

[1] Paul Foucart, *Recherches sur l'origine et la nature des mystères
d'Éleusis*, 1895.

letters, who were moved with admiration for this
land of an ancient civilisation, of magnificent and
imperishable monuments, whose priests had taught
wisdom to the divine Plato. Everything coming
from the Nile became fashionable in Italy—bronzes,
vases, furniture, stuffs, jewellery. Men attempted
to put these objects in a native setting, as can
be seen in the paintings on the walls of Herculaneum and Pompeii. Many of these vividly
coloured frescoes represent an Egyptianised landscape, here a winding river, shaded by palm-trees;
there a bit of country peopled by sphinxes, where
ibises flutter their wings in the sunshine, crocodiles
stretch themselves upon the sand, hippopotamuses
raise their heads from the waters, monkeys climb
along the trees or wrestle with negroes or pigmies.
All these reproductions and reminiscences of Egypt
enjoy a popularity which is only equalled by the
keen interest aroused by the Egyptian religion
itself.

As far back as 105 B.C., we find a Serapeum at
Pouzzoles and an Iseum at Pompeii. Rome had
built a temple to Isis in the time of Sulla.[1]   The
struggle of Antony and Cleopatra against Octavius

[1] *Cf.* G. Lafaye, *Histoire du culte des divinités d'Alex-
andrie*, 1884.   F. Cumont, *Les religions orientales dans
l'empire romain*, 2d ed., 1909.

may have thrown some discredit upon Egyptian cults, for they were forbidden in Rome during the reigns of Augustus and Tiberius. But in 38 A.D. Caligula consecrated the great Roman temple in the Field of Mars to Isis Campensis. Henceforth the Emperors, themselves, set the example of veneration for the goddess, while the legions of Cæsar, the merchants, and the Roman settlers spread the Isiac cult over Africa, Gaul, and Germania,[1] and in every country where the Roman eagle flew. It reached its zenith in the time of the Antonines. ▪In fact, for five hundred years, from the first century B.C., to the fourth A.D., mankind sought for comfort in a system of belief and worship that had originated in Egypt. ▪

Wherein, then, lay the attraction of the Egyptian doctrine? In the first place, in its secret character, in the fact that it was reserved for the initiated. To reveal its mysteries was forbidden.

---

[1] For information regarding relics of the Isiac cult in Europe, see E. Guimet, *L'Isis romaine;* Lafaye, *op. cit.,* p. 162: Ad. Erman, *Aegyptische Religion,* p. 352. The Church of St. Germain-des-Prés in Paris possessed, until the XVIth century, a statuette of Isis; the Church of St. Ursula at Cologne can still boast of a statue of "Isis Unconquered." M. Guimet has gathered together in the Musée Guimet the Isiac objects found in Gaul, and following his initiative, several European museums have searched in their neighbourhood for Isiac figures, hitherto neglected, and have begun a collection.

The two writers, Plutarch and Apuleius,[1] who alone give us any information upon the subject, break off emphatically just at the moment when our curiosity is completely aroused. We gather then very little from their half-revelations about the process of initiation, but fortunately for us the ruins of certain temples, of which the best preserved are at Pompeii, contain representations which enable us to obtain a fairly accurate idea of the religious lives of the Isiacs.

The centre of their life was the Iseum, a temple which in no particular recalls the magnificent Greek remains to be seen in the same region at Pæstum, or in Sicily at Agrigentum and Segesta. Was the Iseum of Pompeii a reproduction, on a smaller scale, of the famous Serapeum of Alexandria, dedicated by Ptolemy Soter to Isis and Serapis? From the description of Rufinus,[2] who

[1] Plutarch, who was high-priest of Apollo at Delphi, at the end of the first century, had dedicated his treatise *De Iside et Osiride* to a priestess of Dionysos, Clea, who was an Isiac. Apuleius has told the story of his initiation into the Mysteries of Isis in Book XI of the *Metamorphoses*, written about 160 A.D.

[2] *Hist. Eccl.*, ii, 23.   *Cf.* Ammien Marcellin, xxii, 17, who extols the magnificent library lodged in an annex of the Serapeum. The following description is by Rufinus, who visited the Serapeum about the end of the fourth century.

"The mound on which it has been built was formed, not by nature, but by the hand of man. It towers above a mass of buildings and is reached by more than one hundred steps. It extends on all sides in a square of great dimensions. All the

Area, Cella, Megarum in the Temple of Isis at Pompeii.

Plate XIII.

visited the Serapeum at the end of the fourth
century, we gather that this monument differed
essentially from the traditional Pharaonic temple
by the greater importance given to those parts
reserved for the priests and worshippers; the shrine
of the god only occupied the central portion; all
around were the buildings used for teaching
purposes and for the contemplative life. The
Serapeum was not only a church; it was also a
convent and a school.

The Iseum of Pompeii did not have these
colossal dimensions. As we know it to-day, it
occupies the site of an older temple, destroyed by
the earthquake of 63, rebuilt before any other in
Pompeii by a zealous community and already in

lower part, up to the level of the pavement, is vaulted. This
basement which receives the light from above through openings,
is divided into secret chambers, separated from one another and
serving divers mysterious functions. The circuit of the upper
story is occupied by conference halls, cells for the pastophori and
a very high building, generally inhabited by the guardians of the
temple and the priests who have taken vows of chastity.—
Behind these buildings, on the inside, cloisters run along the four
sides in a square. In the centre rises the temple, decorated with
columns of precious material and built of magnificent marbles,
employed in profusion. It contains a statue of Serapis, of such
proportions that it can touch one wall with the right and the other
with the left hand. It is affirmed that all kinds of metals and
woods enter into the composition of this colossal figure. The
walls of the sanctuary are reputed to be covered first with plates
of gold, then with plates of silver, and on the outside is a third
layer of bronze for the purpose of protecting the two others. "

use when there occurred the final catastrophe of the year 79.

In the centre of a square court (*area*), surrounded by the ruins of a colonnade, was the sanctuary (*cella*), decorated by a pediment upborne by seven columns and reached by a flight of seven steps. Within the sanctuary is seen a base which served at one and the same time as a pedestal for the statue of Isis and a closet for the storing of the articles used in the service of worship. On the left of the court a large altar and a few smaller ones for sacrifices have been discovered; near at hand is a small square building with a narrow underground passage where two benches are cut in the masonry. This is supposed to have been the *megarum* or probation-hall where the aspirants to initiation slept at night, to be visited by Isis in prophetic dreams. Behind the sanctuary, the outside wall is pierced by five large openings giving access to a larger hall, which is believed to have been the *schola*, a place for meetings, banquets, and the lectures attended by the Isiacs. Adjoining the schola was a vestry with a fountain for purposes of purification. Lastly, between the temple and the neighbouring municipal theatre can be traced the lodgings of the priests, in the remains of a suite of five rooms. (Plate XIII).

If the Iseum of Pompeï was neither Greek nor Pharaonic, perhaps other cities may have possessed temples of the Egyptian type. At Beneventum, a certain Lucilius Labienus erected, in 188 A.D., at his own expense, "an august temple to Isis the Great, mother of the gods, ruler of the Heavens, of the Earth, and of the Nether World, lady of Beneventum. . . ."[1] Of this temple, there remain only the fragments of two red granite obelisks which came from Egypt. Engraved thereon, in bad hieroglyphics, we read the dedication by the donor to Isis, and prayers for the salvation of his Emperor Domitian. May it be that the temple exhibited, along with the obelisks, pylons, hypostyles, a shrine hidden away behind high walls, embedded, as it were in masonry? Perhaps it is only the details that were borrowed from Egypt as an attempt to impart local colour, such as is seen in the temple represented on a fresco at Herculaneum, where sphinxes crouch on either side of the sanctuary door. Moreover, a temple like that of Pompeii was better adapted for the devotional exercises of a religion which fostered continuous communion between the

[1] Concerning the obelisks of Beneventum, see the articles by A. Erman and A. Baillet in *Aegyptische Zeitschrift*, 1896, p. 194, and 1903, p. 147.

goddess and her votaries. In ancient times, a temple was meant to be primarily a place of safety for the statue of the gods; it was the house of the gods before it was a place of worship. The Iseum of Pompeii foreshadows the Christian *ecclesia;* it already provides a large space in which a great assembly of worshippers can gather around a small shrine.

Let us now penetrate, like the initiate, into the temple. The worshipper of Isis rises before dawn to attend the morning service or Isiac matins. The cult has borrowed from the Egyptian ritual its three daily services.[1]  In the Greek and Roman temples, sacrifices were made only upon certain festal days, but here the religious ceremonies were repeated every day. Nor is the worship limited to the monotonous rites of the slaughtering of victims and the consultation of the auspices; a holy drama of divine sacrifice, followed with intense emotion by the people, is actually performed on festal days; on ordinary days it is simply alluded to in the prayers. This drama is the Passion of Osiris.

Let us gaze upon it as though we were the in-

[1] *Décret de Rosette,* éd. Chabas, p. 45.  *Cf.* A. Moret, *Le rituel du culte divin journalier en Égypte,* p. 221.

itiate. The priests await the coming of the congregation. In front stands the high-priest, an ascetic figure with shaven or tonsured crown; his face, too, is smooth, in conformation with the rule for cleanliness imposed by the ritual; he is clad in a linen robe of palest azure hue, which calls to mind the flower of the flax, fruit of the earth, the gift of Isis and Osiris. In order that the body, the abode of the soul, shall be unhampered by matter, in order that he may devote his life to learning, to meditation, and to the teaching of holy things, the high-priest must refrain from all excesses in food and drink.[1] A sacerdotal hierarchy is placed under him, as in Egypt: *prophets*, admitted to intercourse with the gods; *stolists*, priests and priestesses, who robe and disrobe the statues of the gods with stuffs, alternately black and bright to teach us that our knowledge of the gods is half light, half darkness; *pastophori*, who carry, in the processions, the little shrines wherein the holy statuettes dwell and of whom it is said that they guard in their souls, as in a basket, the holy doctrines, pure from all superstition, uncontaminated by any alien influence.[2] These priests of the

[1] Lafaye, *l. c.*, p. 151. The lives of the Isiac priests were so pure that Tertullian proposes them as a model for Christians.

[2] *De Iside et Osiride*, 3–5. In the temples of Isis and of Serapis, there were, moreover, scribes, singers, and musicians, who

second grade are clad in long, light-coloured robes, drawn close about them, leaving the breast, the arms, and the shaven head bare. As they are often Negroes or Egyptians, their dark flesh stands out in bold relief from the light garments. The priestesses wear long, transparent, crinkled robes; their tresses are bound like a diadem upon their brows, and the distinctive feature of their apparel is a fringed scarf, both ends of which are knotted upon the breast (Plate XIV). The stolists of either sex carry a sprinkler or a little vessel, rounded into the semblance of a woman's bosom, because the holy water it contains, purifies, refreshes, and makes mortals divine as does the milk of the goddess Isis[1] (Plate XV). They also shake in their hands the quivering sistrum, emblem of the Egyptian goddesses; its jingling rods lend a rhythm to the movements of the congregation, at the same time repelling Seth, the murderer of Osiris, the evil spirit.

The sistrum signifies, by its quiver, that all beings must be aroused and liberated from the moral and physical state of torpor into which they are ever liable to fall; on the handle of the sistrum, the figures of Isis

---

played on divers flutes, the harp, and the cymbals, and performed special liturgical music (Lafaye, p. 137 *et seq.*).

[1] E. Guimet, *L' Isis romaine;* Apuleius, xi: "Idem gerebat vasculum in modum papillæ rotondatum de quo lacte libebat."

and Nephthys must be engraved as a magic protection, and, if it has four bars, it is because all the movements of matter result from the combination of the four elements, earth, air, fire, water.[1]

These priests, mostly of Egyptian origin, move in appropriate surroundings. The outside walls of the cella, the megarum, the schola are decorated with reliefs or frescoes setting forth legends from Egyptian sources but modified by artists into a composite mythology. Here is Serapis,[2] who has borrowed from Zeus-Jupiter his majestic countenance, yet, between the curls on his forehead, shoot forth the curved horns of the Amon-ram, while his brow is surmounted by a basket (*calathos*), filled with ears of corn, the emblem of abundance. Osiris lies swathed in the funeral shroud, crowned with the high mitre, holding in his crossed fists, the crook and whip, while at his feet is placed a skull, symbol of his lordship over the Nether World. Isis, twice holy, as woman and goddess, reveals her noble and gracious form beneath a transparent raiment; she raises a

---

[1] *De Iside et Osiride*, 63.

[2] Serapis is the State god of the Greek Ptolemaic kings. It has been disputed whether the name and character of this god are of purely Egyptian origin (Osiris-Apis), or whether they are from Sinope or Babylon. M. Isidore Lévy has proved this second theory to be without foundation (*Revue Hist. des Religions*, 1910).

sistrum and clasps the cross of life (Fig. 9); Isis mother, holds in her lap the infant, Horus, who carries his finger to his lips[1] in an attitude that has become traditional in the representations of the Madonna and the infant Jesus. Farther on is Anubis, leader of the souls, who holds erect his dog-like head above a close-fitting Roman tunic; Thot, the ibis stalks along on the slender legs of his tribe, a monster with the head of a lion and the body of a hippopotamus, the "Devourer" of the Egyptian texts, which swallows the wicked in the other world, and opens its large jaws to carry out the sentence of the Osirian tribunal. Seth-Typhon, grim and hieratic, takes his place among the luminous gods, even as night attends on day. Into this procession of gods of the Osirian legend are introduced other figures from the Greek mythology.[2]

[1] The interpretation of this gesture in Græco-Roman times is that Horus raises a finger to his mouth to command the silence which is due to the mysteries. It is more probable that originally the gesture alluded rather to the creative power of the divine Word. Cf. E. Guimet, Plutarque et l' Égypte.

[2] In the megarum of Pompeii, plaster bas-reliefs represent Ares and Aphrodite, Hermes and a nymph, surrounded by little cupids with various attributes; in the dwellings of the priests were seen Dionysos, Narcissus, Chiron instructing Achilles; in the schola were two large pictures of the abduction of Io, who was identified, because of her cow-shape, with Isis-Hathor, and the arrival of the goddess in Egypt. In the megarum and the cella, a series of plaster medallions set forth the various attributes of the Isiac

Roman Isis.
(Musée du Capitole).
Plate XIV

Such is the scenery of the Isiac matins which are now about to begin. While the congregation gathers in the front of the sanctuary, the high-priest, clad in white raiment, mounts the steps and draws apart the white curtains[1] and reveals to their eyes the awful image of the goddess. [ The statue found at Pompeii is of marble, painted and gilded. The goddess stands erect, her legs close in the customary hieratic attitude; her right arm, as far as the elbow, clings to her side; the fore-arm is raised and holds the sistrum, the left arm hangs down beside her body and clasps the handled cross ¥, the emblem of life. The hair, formerly gilded, is separated into many slender braids, some fall about her shoulders, the others are gathered about her brow to form a coronet which is wrought with flowers. The colour of the trans-parent clinging robe is red, its edges trimmed with

---

cult, mingled with interlaced foliage. There were seen in succession, the eagle of the Ptolemies; a bull's skull, recalling the sacrificial animal; a radiating uræus; a flying bird; a dwarf gladiator; the typhonian animal seated and snapping his jaws; a symbolic figure which looks like a fœtus surrounded by ears of corn; a vessel in which Isis carried Nile water; and finally the sistrum which the goddess shakes (cf. Mazois, xi, Pl. 4; Guzman, Pompeii, p. 87).

[1] It is the apertio templi, "the opening of the temple" (Apuleius, xii). In the Egyptian ritual, "the opening of the doors of the shrine" was welcomed by hymns which have been preserved (A. Moret, Rituel du culte divin, p. 67).

embroidery of gold.
Round her neck is a
broad necklace from
which small pendants
fall, those on the
breast are in the form
of a moon-crescent
and a star. A girdle
gathers the robe be-
neath her breast, its
clasp adorned with
two crocodile heads,
the crocodile being
the typhonian animal
subject to the goddess
(Fig. 9).

Before the image,
thus revealed, the
priests pour libations
of holy water, sup-
posed to
come from
the Nile,[1]

FIG. 9.—The Statue of Isis in the Temple at and sprinkle
Pompeii.
(*Real Museo Borbonico*, t. xiv, pl. 35.)     the congre-

[1] Commentary of Servius upon the *Æneid*, iv, 512: "In
templo Isidis aqua sparsa de Nilo esse dicebatur."

gation; the sacred fire is then prepared so that, according to Egyptian ritual, the sanctuary may be purified by fire and water. Next, the high-priest, standing on the threshold of the cella, awakens the goddess, addressing her in the Egyptian language;[1] at his bidding, she arouses from her slumber, compelled to obey the priest who knows her true name.[2] The tribute of burnt-offering is offered up upon the altars and with voices upraised in song, the servants of the faith salute the first hour of the day.

It was probably at this first service that the stolists robed the image of the goddess and arranged her hair according to the rite described by Apuleius, in the procession of *Navigium Isidis*. It was the duty of the women to present to the goddess a mirror and pins wherewith to secure her hair. The raiment of the goddess varied according to the festivals, but it generally retained one characteristic (Plate XIV), the fringed scarf fastened on the breast in what was called the Isiac knot.[3] Finally the statue was adorned with jewels, then a sistrum and a golden vessel were placed in its hands. How tawdry become our

[1] Porphyrius, *De abstinentia*, iv, 9. *Cf.* Cumont, *loc. cit.*, pp. 143 and 344 (τῶν Αἰγυπτίων φωνῇ ἐγείρει τόν Θεόν).

[2] For the magic power of the "name" see A. Moret: *In the Time of the Pharaohs*, p. 290.

[3] Apuleius, *Metamorphoses*, xi, 4.    H. E. Butler's translation.

Madonnas of Italy and Spain if compared with this gorgeous and radiant image that delighted the eyes of all who gazed upon it.   The Isis discovered at Cadiz[1] wore a diadem heavy with pearls, emeralds, carbuncles, hyacinths, and crystals of flint. In her ears, two pearls and two emeralds glistened; the same stones sparkled on her bosom, upon her wrists and ankles; two diamond rings blazed upon her little finger, while the other fingers shone with pearls and emeralds.   The inventory of the temples of Isis, discovered at Nemi, gives us a detailed list of all the articles of attire and adornment that went to make the image of the goddess a splendid vision, and we understand how she so dazzled her adorers that after the service had ended they would "tarry in the temple" to worship her "to the full of their heart's delight."

The temple remained open, and about two o'clock in the afternoon the songs of the priests called the people to a second service, which might be styled the Vespers of Isis.  We do not know what ceremonies were then performed; we only know that much time was devoted to contemplation and meditation before the sacred images. There is a fresco in Herculaneum that portrays for us the adoration of a vessel said to contain

[1] *Cf.* Lafaye, pp. 135–137.

Nile water, one of the many symbols of Osiris (Plate XVI, 1). The high-priest, turning his back to the cella and facing the congregation, raises the sacred chalice to the level of his chest and offers it for their adoration. The worshippers form two groups, one on either side of a smoking altar, and they sing while shaking their sistrums to the accompaniment of the flute.[1]

A short service closed the day. The sanctuary was purified with burning kyphi,[2] and the statue was disrobed for the night; the curtains were drawn and the goddess was left to sleep till morning. To the devotees of both sexes had been granted the ecstatic joy of spending long hours face to face with the divinity. "What we most desire of the gods is to know them," wrote Plutarch[3] to the high-priestess Clea; in like manner, many centuries earlier, the Egyptian worshipper yearned for no greater happiness than "to behold the god in his fair festivities of the earth and heaven."

[1] The plan, decoration, and frescoes of the Iseum of Pompeii described here can be seen reproduced in the Isiac Gallery in the Musée Guimet, Paris.

[2] According to Plutarch, *De Iside et Osiride*, 80–81, resin was burnt in the morning, myrrh at noon, and kyphi at the evening service. The daily cult also included three sacrifices to the Sun (52) made in the course of the day, as in the Egyptian temples.

[3] *De Iside et Osiride*, 1.

This daily worship was nevertheless but the humblest manifestation of the piety of the Isiacs. On certain festival days, all the mysterious figures described above, which enlivened the walls of the temple, all those emblematic instruments, full of secret significance, which excited the curiosity of the profane and haunted the minds of the initiated, seemed to detach themselves from the walls and descend as tangible apparitions into the temple. Those ibises, an exotic inanimate fiction, upon the walls, behold! they come to motion and stalk live birds, with stately tread, around the slender palm-trees transplanted inside the temple; and a procession advances, composed of priests and priestesses, masked in the  semblance of gods and strange animals,[1] tricked out in symbolic attires, and bearing quaint emblems; but as it moves for-

---

[1] The Egyptian priests and sometimes the Pharaohs (Diodorus, i, 62) put on these masks in processions or ceremonies in the temples (cf. Mariette, *Denderah*, iv, Plate 31).    In Rome characteristic incidents occurred.    In 43 B.C., the ædile, M. Volusius, wishing to leave the town without being known, borrowed from one of his friends, an Isiac initiate, a wooden head of the dog Anubis, and wearing it, walked through the streets, gesticulating and employing all the mimicry used in the celebration of the Mysteries (V. Maximus, vii, 3, 8).    The Emperor Commodus followed one day a procession of Isiacs with shaved head and carrying in his arms an image of the dog Anubis, repeatedly causing the idol to fall over and knock with its muzzle upon the head of the priests (Lampridus, *Commodus*, ix).    *Cf.* Lafaye, *op. laud.*, pp. 46 and 62.

ward, with rhythmic tread, to the music of a march
—whereof, surely, Mozart caught the echo when he
wrote the *Magic Flute*,—are they not the very gods
and goddesses themselves, become incarnate for
the benefit of man?    The Egyptian ritual delights
in this twofold presentment, symbolic and tangible,
of the doctrines.    The Osiris myth conjured up
daily in the prayers is, on feast-days, actualised,
made manifest to the senses as a true vision never
more to be forgotten; as a pageant of the dolorous
events, the awful mysteries of the Passion of Osiris.

What were these festivals?    The most important
occurred in the spring and autumn.    The life
of the gods blooms and fades with the seasons.
The death and renewal of plants, the rising and
setting of the sun call to mind the death and
resurrection of Osiris.

They say that Osiris is buried when they put the
seed in the ground, that he is born again and comes
back to the earth when the seeds begin to sprout;
that is why Isis brings forth Horus-the-Child (Har-
pocrates) about the time of the winter solstice; after
the spring equinox a festival is celebrated to commemorate the maternity of Isis.[1]

Apuleius has given us a vivid description of the
spring festival which he witnessed at Cenchreæ,

[1] *De Iside et Osiride*, 65, 70.

one of the three seaports of Corinth, and which
was called the Festival of the Ship of Isis (*Isidis
Navigium*).[1] It took place on the 5th of March,
when the winter winds having ceased, the sea is
again open for navigation. It was natural that in
countries bordering on the Mediterranean, the
festival of the spring should become a festival of
the sea. I must refer the reader to Apuleius[2]
for the picturesque details of the procession, which
I mention here only on account of its significance.
At the vanguard of the procession, the populace
disported itself in many a merry guise, in a spirit
of carnival frolic. Then came the retinue of Isis
itself, in successive grades of nobility—musicians,
choir, the initiated, priests—typifying the mysteries as they gain in purity and elevation in passing
from the minds of the common folk to the minds
of the chosen few. Last of all came the gods, in
the form of venerable images or allegorical objects
borne aloft upon the shoulders of the chief dignitaries, and at the end of the procession appeared
the emblem of Isis, a small golden urn, with a
handle coiled into a uræus (*cf.* Plate XV), containing the holy water, substance and symbol of

---

[1] *Metamorphoses*, ix; *cf.* Lafaye, *l. c.*, p. 121.
[2] See Apuleius, *Metamorphoses*, Book XI, in the excellent
translation of H. E. Butler, Oxford, Clarendon Press, 1910.

Osiris.[1] When the procession reaches the sea-shore, the high-priest purifies the vessel according to the ritual, dedicates it to Isis, and the votive ship, built of precious material, and laden with offerings, is launched.[2]

The autumn festival was, however, still more important because at that time there was a representation of the death and resurrection of Osiris. On the 13th of November, which corresponds to the 17th Athyr of the Egyptian calendar, Osiris fell a victim to the murderer Seth-Typhon. On an improvised stage in the temple, the priests, clad, as we have seen, in the garb of the gods, performed a masque, the Osirian mystery. Though the texts we possess give us no very clear information, it is certain that the murder of Osiris was realistically represented—the launching on the Nile of the chest containing his body; the wailings and quest of Isis, searching the depths of the water, wandering even to Byblos to recover the body and bring it back to Egypt.[3] The audience mingled

[1] Cf. *De Iside et Osiride*, 36. The Egyptian vessel is also a symbol of Osiris. *Cf.* Lanzone, *Dizionario di mitologia egizia*, Plate CCXCIV.

[2] A similar fête of the sea is still, in our day, celebrated at Catania in Sicily (*cf.* Lafaye, p. 126; Cumont, p. 345).

[3] The return of Isis from Phœnicia was commemorated in a special festival in December, the 7th Tybi. Plutarch describes some features of the ceremony: "When the nights becoming

their tears with the woeful lamentations of the goddess. "They imitated the gesticulations of a mother overcome with grief."[1] The quest was so thrilling, the wailings so piercing, that they annoyed the public outside the temple, and Ovid is greatly provoked by "this god whom they have never finished seeking."[2] An inscription, dating from the beginning of our era, tells us that at Gallipoli the episode of Isis was performed on a body of water that was called the Nile, the initiated acting the parts of pilots and searchers, sailing to and fro upon the water and letting down nets into it.[3] Isis appeared, mourning and in

longer increased the darkness and caused the light to wane rapidly, the priests were wont, in one of many mournful ceremonies, to throw over a golden bull a black covering of linen fabric, by reason of the mourning of the goddess, and they exposed it to the public throughout four consecutive days, from the 17th of the month (of Athyr), because they regard the bull as the living image of Osiris.

"These four days of mourning have each their meaning. On the first day, they mourn for the falling of the waters of the Nile and their return to their channel; on the second, for the flight of the North winds compelled to give up their sway to the South wind (the Simoon); on the third, for the decline of day which has become shorter than night; on the fourth, for the bare condition of the earth after the trees are bereft of their foliage. . . . (De Iside, 39). "When the time has come for the funeral of Osiris, the priests cut wood with which to make a chest in the shape of a crescent moon. . . ." (De Iside, 41).

[1] Minutius Felix, Octav., 21.
[2] Metam., ix, 692: "Nunquam satis quæsitus Osiris."
[3] Paul Foucart, Mystères d'Éleusis, p. 37. Lafaye quotes an

tears; she sought her husband's remains, and as she found them she put them aside with care, all the time hiding herself from the eyes of Seth.[1]

When all the fragments of the divine body had been recovered, the mournful dirges of this Festival of All the Dead were turned into songs of joy. It was on the third day that Osiris had been found (*Osiris inventus*) and had risen again (*Osiris ex se natus*).[2] "On the night of the 19th day of Athyr (15th November), the priests go down to the seashore, bearing in a sacred ark a golden vessel which they fill with sweet water. Then all the assembly raise their voices and cry that Osiris is risen." Sometimes, a priest in the garb of Anubis comes forward at this moment, leading a little child by the hand; this is the newborn Osiris.[3] Another rite which illustrates the resurrection is described at Denderah. "They mixed earth with sweet water, spices, and grains of wheat and barley; from this paste they fashioned a little figure in the form of a crescent, dressed, and adorned it."[4] The Egyptian texts explain that

---

Ephesian inscription which seems to refer to a similar rite in Isis worship (p. 144).

[1] *De Iside et Osiride*, 59.
[2] Lafaye, *l. c.*, p. 127, n. 8.   Juvenal, *Sat.*, viii, 29.
[3] Lactantius, *Divin. Institut.*, L. 21.
[4] *De Iside et Osiride*, 39; *cf.* 52.   See *ante*, p. 81.

this figure was buried and that, when the grains of wheat and barley sprouted in the springtime, Osiris was manifestly born again.

The resurrection of Osiris was commemorated by great rejoicings (*hilaria*), during which the Isiacs filled the streets and public places, an object of shame and disgust to some of the population, an amusing, delightful sight to others. The initiated assembled at a banquet (*cœna Serapiaca*).[1] Sometimes games were held in a circus. Is it perhaps a sacred entertainment of this kind that is represented in one of the frescoes at Herculaneum? On a stage in a theatre, or it may be in the temple, a negro, crowned with reeds and lotus flowers, performs a step dance, resting one hand on his hip, while he gesticulates with the other. Priests and priestesses give a rhythmic accompaniment to his dance, upon the flute and the jingling sistrum[2] (Plate XVI, 2).

Can it be wondered at, that such pageants appealed to the popular imagination? The great changes of nature were presented in the shape of a

---

[1] Tertullian, i, 474.

[2] Pausanias (x, 32, 12) also describes two festivals, of the spring and autumn, which were celebrated in the temple of Isis of Tithorea in Phocis. In Rome, the Isiacs marched in processions along the streets and paused at certain temporary altars called *pausæ*. *Cf.* Lafaye, *l. c.*, p. 128.

human drama; Osiris died as all men die, but he was born again, in order to teach men how they too might enter upon a new life; the death and rebirth of the god, corresponding to the changes of the seasons, aroused in the hearts of believers similar feelings of joy and sorrow. But the inner meaning escaped the majority of the spectators; it was the initiated alone, who fully understood it; the pathetic legend of Osiris opened the way of a virtuous life and a happy death; it provided man with an example for his own destiny.

How did one become an initiate and what were the mysteries disclosed to the happy few?[1] Apuleius, in the *Metamorphoses*, recounting his dedication to the goddess, reveals little of the mysteries, but he gives some very precious information concerning the state of mind of the neophyte and the different stages of probation through which he passes. The hero of the novel, Lucius, in whom we recognise Apuleius himself, has led a dissipated life and has been changed into an ass by a witch. But during the Festival of the Ship of Isis (*Navigium Isidis*), already referred to, the good goddess is so touched by his sorrows and his remorse, that she restores him to his human shape, but, only on

---

[1] The *Initiati* or *Isiaci* formed colleges (*collegia Isidis*) over which presided a Father or Mother (*Pater, Mater sacrorum*).

condition, that Lucius enrols himself in her "sacred soldiery"[1] and dedicates to her the remainder of his life.

Lucius tries, loyally, to keep his promise. He rents a cell in the precincts of the temple,[2] and attends the daily services of the goddess, listens to the teaching given from the pulpit,[3] lives in intercourse with the priests, and worships the goddess unceasingly; every night he sees her in his dream and is admonished by her to become initiated into her mysteries. But the strict rúles of the faith, the obligations of chastity and abstinence, hold him back. At last, touched by the grace of

[1] The Isiac, like the initiate to the rites of Mithra, called himself a "soldier of the god"; the Christians also are styled "soldiers of Christ."

[2] In imitation of the great Serapeum in Alexandria, the Isiac temples in Europe had chambers, or were connected with buildings, in which the candidates to initiation confined themselves, like Apuleius, during the time of their novitiate, "under a voluntary yoke of service." In Egypt, at the time of the Ptolemies this novitiate was rigorous. The neophytes who submitted to living as recluses (κάτοχοι) in the prison (κατοχή) of the temple, would sometimes await for ten, twelve, or sixteen years, the consecration of that baptism which would restore them to liberty and worldly life. See Reitzenstein, *Die Hellenistischen Mysterien religionen* (1910), pp. 72–80.

[3] According to Apuleius, there was in the temple of Cenchreæ a hall in which the people assembled in congregation (*concio*) and the Isiac priest preached to them from a pulpit (*suggestus*). These statements are of great importance as they manifest a revolution in the religious practice; the Greek and Roman worships do not include any teaching, and the temples do not exhibit any pulpits.

·the goddess, he entreats the high-priest to initiate him into the secrets of the Holy Night[1] (*ut me noctis sacratæ tandem arcanis initiaret*).   But the priest, without discouraging him, warns him not to be over-eager, "neither to delay when summoned, nor to hasten unbidden."   "The goddess herself would call him at the appointed time; in her hands are the keys of Hell and the way of salvation; the act of dedication was regarded as a voluntary death, followed by a new birth and the entering upon a new life.   Therefore, he must await the day ordained by the goddess."   Excited by the deferment, Lucius, more sedulous than ever, attends the services and prepares himself by fasting for the holy probation.   At length comes a night, when the goddess warns him that the moment of his long desire has arrived; she decrees the amount he must pay for the cost of his reception and ordains that the high-priest become his god-father.[2]

On the same day, after morning service, the high-priest brings forth from a secret place in the

---

[1] In Egypt, also, the Mystery of Osiris was performed at night (Herodotus, ii, 60).   The secret rites lasted throughout twenty-four hours, and are "the vigil of the twelve hours of the day and the twelve hours of the night" (Junker, *Die Stundenwachen* . . . . 1910).

[2] Or, more exactly, his "father."   The Ptolemaic κάτοχοι use the same expression to designate the priest who initiates them.

shrine, certain books written in an unknown script
—in hieroglyphics—and reads them to the neophyte. Lucius, escorted by a band of the initiated, is led to the baths, near by, where he is
immersed in the font (*lavacrum*) and undergoes
the rite of *baptism*.[1] The high-priest, after prayer
to the gods, causes the water to flow over him on
all sides, according to the Egyptian ritual. Then
Lucius is led back to the temple, where he casts
himself at the feet of the goddess. The high-
priest secretly confides to him certain ineffable
words, and, openly, bids him to abstain, for ten
consecutive days, from the pleasures of the table,
eating nothing that has had life, and drinking no
wine.

After ten days spent in ascetic meditation,
Lucius is led back to the temple, "with westward
sloping sun." The initiated welcome him with
various gifts;[2] then the uninitiated are dismissed.
The high-priest clothes Lucius in a linen robe and
takes him to the very heart of the sanctuary.
Here Apuleius breaks off, leaving our curiosity
unsatisfied:

[1] This word is used in the Ptolemaic papyri and is applied to
the recluses of the Serapeum who receive initiation (Reitzenstein, *loc. cit.*, p. 77).

[2] Reitzenstein suggests that the neophyte receives offerings
because baptism has already made him a god.

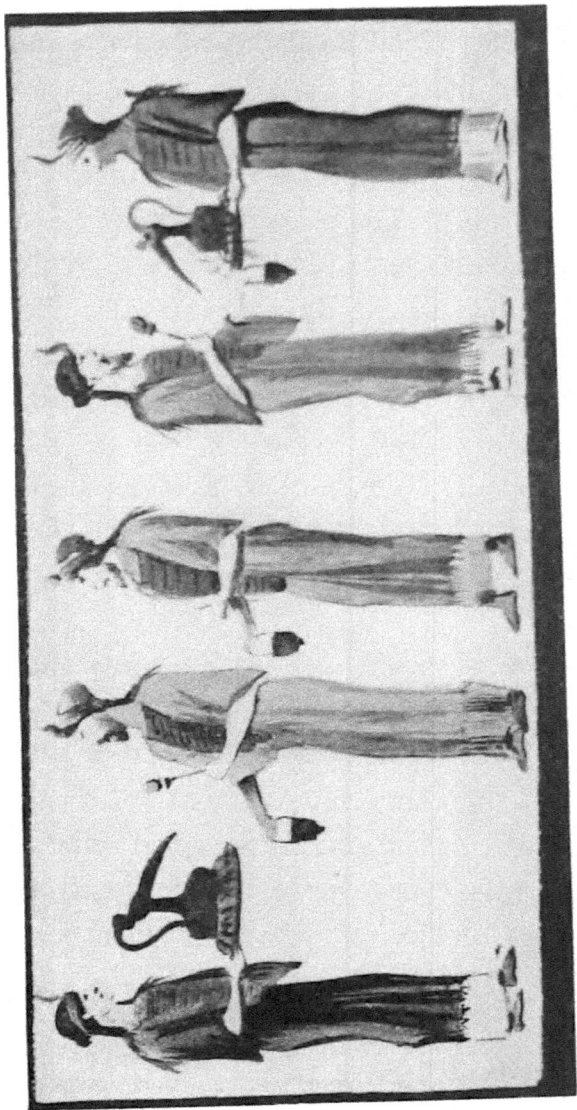

Isiaques Carrying the Hydria-Vessel, the Vessel in the Form of a Woman's Breast and the Sprinkler.
(E. Guimet, *L'Isis romaine*).
Plate XV.

Perchance, eager reader, thou burnest to know what then was said, what done. I would tell thee, were it lawful for me to tell, and thou shouldst know all, were it lawful for thee to hear. But both tongue and ear would be infected with like guilt, did I gratify such rash curiosity. Yet since, perchance, it is pious craving that vexes thee, I will not torment thee by prolongation of thy anguish. Hear, then, and believe, for what I tell is true. I drew nigh to the confines of death. I trod the threshold of Proserpine, I was borne through all the elements and returned to earth again. I saw the sun gleaming with bright splendour at dead of night; I approached the gods above and the gods below, and worshipped them face to face. Behold, I have told thee things of which, though thou hast heard them, thou must yet know naught.[1]

At break of day, Lucius, who has put on and taken off in succession twelve different robes, now arrayed in a cloak embroidered with figures of beasts, bearing in his hand a flaming torch, wearing a crown of white palm leaves, which radiate from his head like the sun, is led to a wooden dais in front of the statue of the goddess. The people throng in all the spaces around the shrine. Suddenly, the curtains are drawn aside and he appears in the garb and attitude that symbolise the sun.

This "birthday of his initiation" is celebrated

[1] *Metamorphoses*, xi, 23.   H. E. Butler's translation.

by three days of festival and banqueting; Lucius
still remains in the temple, enjoying ineffable
ecstasy in the contemplation of the goddess. At
length he withdraws, after having sung to the
goddess a litany of rhythmic verses,[1] and having
offered to the high-priest gifts and kisses. Later,
Lucius undergoes further initiations; he is admitted
to the mysteries of Osiris, to the nocturnal orgies
of Serapis, and thus receives three successive revelations. Finally, he is chosen to be one of the
Pastophori, and, not without pride, he now shows
his tonsured head in all the processions of Isis,
performing the duties "of that most ancient
company of priests, established in the great days
of Sylla."[2]

Is it possible for us to arrive at some idea of
what Apuleius was unable to reveal to the profane
reader: the Mysteries of the Holy Vigil?    Apuleius
states that the neophyte was invited to *hear* and
to *see* secret things.   In the Mysteries of Eleusis,
also, the aspirants to initiation witnessed dramatic
scenes, looked on pictures, or listened to revela-

---

[1] Lafaye has succeeded in arranging in verse the rhythmical
prose of this passage of Apuleius which strongly recalls the
litanies which in later times were composed in honour of the
Virgin (p. 138).
[2] *Metamorphoses*, xi, 30.   H. E. Butler's translation.

tions.[1] Then, Apuleius saw, perhaps he himself
assisted in a few scenes chosen from a sacred
drama,[2] or a mystery; what he heard was the explanation of these scenes and the revelation of
their symbolic meaning.

Apuleius names the successive episodes of this
drama without describing them: *baptism, death*, and
*rebirth; descent into Hell; transfiguration into the
Sun.* He thus gives us, as it were, an argument,
or a heading to sum up each scene. Fortunately,
these headings refer to rites which are clearly
Egyptian. So, calling to my aid certain hieroglyphic evidence, I shall try to supply the text
missing between the headings.

The neophyte receives at first a baptism which

[1] Paul Foucart (*Mystères d'Éleusis*, p. 45) has established that
the Eleusinian Mysteries included: (1) processions; (2) exhibitions
of pictures or dramatic scenes; (3) oral explanation. I find that
the Isiac Mysteries move within the same frame.

[2] Clement of Alexandria uses this expression for the rites of
Eleusis, δρᾶμα μυστικόν (*Prostr.*, ii, p. 12, ed. Pot.) Also
Plutarch clearly states that in the Mysteries of Isis the sufferings
of Osiris were represented in mimic form and had a symbolic
meaning: "Isis would not that her own woes and grievous journeyings, that the deeds of his wisdom and heroism should fall
into oblivion and silence. She instituted holy, sacred Mysteries
(τελεταί), which would afford an image, a representation in mimic
scenes of the sufferings he endured (εἰκόνας καὶ ὑπονοίας καὶ μίμημα
τῶν τότε παθημάτων), that they might serve as a pious teaching
and a consolatory hope to the men and women who passed
through the same hardships."

cleanses his body and his soul.   The water, which
was supposed to come from the Nile, makes of him,
what it makes of every dead Egyptian who receives
the rite, the equal of Osiris,   Like the god, he is
supposed to die to all things of the earth but to be
born again into a new life.[1]   Baptism is called by
Tertullian, also, a symbol of death, and St. Paul
wrote: "Know ye not, that so many of us as were
baptised into Jesus Christ were baptised into his
death?   Therefore, we are buried with him by
baptism into death; that like as Christ was raised
up from the dead by the glory of the Father, even
so we also should walk in newness of life."[2]   The
apologist Firmicus Maternus, jeering at the Mysteries of Isis, sets this baptism over against that of the
Christians: "In vain deemest thou that this water
worshipped by thee, can save thee.   It is another
water which makes men to be born anew."[3]   The
controversy is valuable to us, for it teaches us what
the Christians denied to the Isiac baptism, and
what the Isiacs expected from it.

After baptism, the neophyte now identified with

[1] *Cf.* Junker, *Die Stundenwachen in den Osirismysterien,* pp.
67–102.                                      [2] Romans vi, 3, 4.
[3] *De errore prof. relig.,* 2, 5: "*Frustra tibi hanc aquam, quam
colis, putas aliquando prodesse.   Alia est aqua, qua renovati homines
renascuntur.*"   *Cf.* Tertullian, *De præscriptione hæretic.,* xli.

Osiris, has to take part in a representation of his own death and resurrection. The priest says to Lucius that "the very act of dedication is a voluntary death and an imperilling of life"; and Lucius adds: "I drew nigh to the confines of death." What kind of death? It cannot mean the punishment incurred in ancient times by any man who in order to satisfy a sacrilegious curiosity tries to see the gods. Lucius, called by Isis, has nothing to fear from her. The death which awaits him is purely symbolic; it is the ritual death of the Egyptian worship. Only those who have been mutilated like Osiris, and who have received the rites invented by Isis can enjoy the bliss of a second life.

I presume, therefore, that the high-priest led the novice to a dark chamber, staged and arranged in conformity with the customary externals of funeral scenes. There, the neophyte had to gaze upon paintings or bas-reliefs, or living pictures setting forth the death of Osiris, the dismemberment of his corpse, and the reconstitution of his body; upon the magic rites performed by Isis and Nephthys, assisted by Thot and Anubis; finally upon the resurrection of Osiris and his fusion with the Sun Râ. So far, there is nothing with which the postulant would not be perfectly familiar. The factor that made these scenes new, conferring upon them the character of a revelation, was the commentary of the priest. He set forth the ethical and practical value of these rites when applied to individual man. Osiris had called all men of "good will" to become his liegemen, to share the benefit of his passion; the powerful rites which had delivered him from the bonds of death would also, if correctly applied, deliver all men from physical death. Once identified with Osiris, the postulant had therefore to be mutilated as the god had been, in order to obtain salvation. After having *seen* and *heard*, he agreed in an outburst of faith, to accept all the consequences of his initiation. How far the Osirian death was actualised on his own body, it is difficult to guess. Is it possible to imagine that the neophyte lay upon a funeral couch, undergoing the simulation of mutilation without apprehension? In Egypt, these rites were performed not only upon the statues of the gods and upon human mummies, but also upon the very person of the living King. When Pharaoh was adored, as god, in the temple, it was supposed that his perishable body had undergone ritual death, had been dismembered and reconstituted, in order that it might be endowed with divine life. Egypt thus offered two examples of the application of

Osirian death to men; the cult of the dead and the cult of the Pharaoh during his life.[1]   It was Isis who devised "that remedy that gives immortality"; therefore, the initiated to the Isiac mysteries received, in their lifetime, the promises of a future bliss, but upon the condition that they should undergo Osirian death, or, at least, an imitation of it.   This test made the postulant not only an equal of Osiris, but a new Osiris; even as the god would live eternally,[2] so would the initiate live eternally after his death.   And even as in Egypt, any dead man, consecrated by the rites, usually assumes the name and appears in the rôle and garb of Osiris, even so did the Isiac initiate cause himself to be portrayed in the garb and with the attributes of Serapis.[3]

The novice, after passing through the gates of death "was reborn" and henceforth counted the day of his initiation as the first of his real life.

[1] A. Moret, *Du caractère religieux de la royauté pharaonique*, p. 217.

[2] In the Phrygian Mysteries in which Attis plays the same part that Osiris does in the Isiac rites, the people sang: "Have confidence, O mysts! for the god is saved and salvation will also spring for you from out your misery."   *Cf.* with Paul's Epistle to the Romans vi., 5: "If we have been planted together in the likeness of his death, we shall be also in the likeness of his resurrection."   The Egyptian formula occurs in *Pyr. of Ounas*, l. 240.

[3] F. Cumont, *l. c.*, p. 278, note 76.

How was this rebirth actualised?    The neophyte
put on a shining garment, bright as the day, to
resemble the resurrected Osiris.[1]    The raiment
symbolised his *"glorious"* body issuing from its
mortal coil.    Was there no allegory behind?    Let
us go back to those sacred books in Egyptian
script, from which Lucius received his instruction.

What knowledge did they impart?    Probably
this:    In Egypt, in order to represent gestation
and rebirth, either a statue or the mummy of the
deceased was placed inside the hide of a sacrificed
animal or inside a wooden cow; or, a priest would
lay himself down within the hide on the night of
the funeral, as a substitute for the dead man.[2]
Next morning, the priest was considered to issue
from the skin as from a womb.    Mythology
coming to the aid of magic, the deceased became
identified with the Sun Râ, born under the form
of a calf from the cow Nouit, who was goddess of
Heaven.[3]    Both Plutarch (52) and Apuleius[4]
mention the wooden image of a cow, which was
borne upon the priest's shoulders in the procession

---

[1] *De Iside et Osiride*, 78; *Metamorphoses*, xi, 29.

[2] Herodotus, ii, 129, 132.    Diodorus, i, 85.    *Cf.* V. Loret,
*Les fêtes d'Osiris au mois de Choïak*, ap. *Recueil*, iv, p. 26.    See
also what has been written above, p. 86.

[3] A. Moret, *Du caractère religieux de la royauté pharaonique*, p.
217, n. I.                                                    [4] (xi, 10.)

of Isis. Did the wooden cow mean for the Isiacs what it meant for the Egyptians, the "womb" from which the dead are born anew? Judging from the episode of Aristæus in the *Georgics*,[1] the Romans were acquainted with the rite of the hide. Virgil gives to the bee-breeders a recipe which will bring about spontaneous generation of bees. By the action of magic rites, a swarm can be brought into existence within the hides of sacrificed bulls. This miraculous process, as the Latin writers knew,[2] was derived from Egyptian and Orphic traditions. On the other hand, the Egyptians were familiar also with the idea that the soul issued from the skin of victims under the form of a bee.[3] Was this tradition, which Virgil presents in a popular form, propounded to the neophyte with its mystic significance? At any rate, the presence on the walls of the megarum of a bee and a fœtus surrounded with ears of corn suggests that those symbols were in some way or other employed to illustrate the mysteries of new birth.[4]

---

[1] *Georgics*, iv, 281 and 556.

[2] Commentary of Servius on the *Georgics*, iii, 364: "*Haec . . . ex Ægyptiis tracta sunt sacris.*"

[3] Tomb of Seti I, ed. Lefébure, part 3, Pl. 3, l. 48. *Cf.* Lefébure, *L'office des morts à Abydos*, and Ph. Virey, *Quelques observations sur l'épisode d'Aristée*, 1889.

[4] The worship of Mithra has also a rite of rebirth called taurobolium: the myst outstretched in a pit, simulating the tomb,

After the funeral rites are accomplished, the neophyte is said "to tread the threshold of Proserpina" (*calcato Proserpinæ limine*). In other words, he descends into Hell. The theme, probably derived from the Egyptians,[1] had been familiar to all since the time of Homer and Virgil. In the Orphic rites, inspired by Egypt, the initiate receives a holy book which shall teach him the right ways to Hades. In the Eleusinian Mysteries, the descent into Hell, after the ceremony of ritual death, is made amid surroundings which conjure up alternately the fearful depths of Hades or the pleasant stretches of the Elysian Fields.

The soul at the moment of death experiences the same sensations as those experience who are initiated into great mysteries. Word and thing are alike: we say τελευτᾶν (to die) and τελεῖσθαι (to be initiated). There are, at first, steps to be taken at random, painful wanderings astray from the right path, anxious and unavailing journeys through the darkness. Then, before the end, the crisis of fear, the shudder, the shiver, the cold sweat, the terror. But afterwards, a marvellous light breaks upon the eyes;

receives gory baptism from a bleeding bull slaughtered above his head; he exposes his face and all the parts of his body to the streaming blood and even drinks of it. The myst is said to be born anew from this baptism of blood, to be purified from his sins for an eternal life, *in æternum renatus*. *Cf.* Cumont, *l. c.*, p. 100.

[1] Suetonius (*Caligula*, 57) states that even in the theatre the descent into Hell was produced on the stage by Egyptian actors.

the soul enters into pure regions, and meadows echoing with the sound of voices and of dances; sacred utterances, divine apparitions inspire the soul with awe.

Was the descent into Hell in the Holy Vigil interpreted in the same way as by the Egyptian? Was the neophyte, like the Egyptian dead, called before an Osirian tribunal, and was his conscience weighed in the balance against Justice and Truth? The texts suggest no answer, but the tribunal in the Nether World was a theme often treated by the Roman poets, especially Virgil, Horace, and Ovid.[1]  It must also have been familiar to the Isiacs, be it only through the Roman channel. Besides, the megarum of Pompeii affords, in favour of this hypothesis, a valuable testimony: the presence, among the plaster reliefs found there, of the "Devourer," the Egyptian monster, which devours the guilty cast out by the Osirian Justice. . May we not infer that the tribunal of Osiris was one of the scenes or pictures shown to the initiate? As to the secrets confided to him by the priest, they were perhaps the powerful formulæ which facilitated the deceased Egyptian in his justification.[2]  Furthermore, the ethical standard of the worshippers of Isis, according to Plutarch and

[1] See above p. 130.
[2] Cf. *In the Time of the Pharaohs*, Ch. "Book of the Dead."

Apuleius, their observance of a temperate life, their love of fair dealing, their thirst for truth, are all merits likewise advanced by the deceased Egyptian as claims to a favourable verdict from the Osirian tribunal.

The neophyte, exalted by ten days of fasting and meditation, was probably less sensitive to the puerile mimicry or the conventional stagery of the rites, than amazed and impressed by the sublime significance of the Osirian death, instrument of redemption, promise of immortality. Besides, the surroundings now become more cheerful. Leaving the dismal crypt, where he had experienced the pangs of death, he was introduced to another chamber, where Isis, clad in white raiment, sparkling with jewels, welcomed him maternally. Suddenly a disc of beaming rays illuminated the room. Lucius "saw at dead of night the sun glowing with splendour."[1] It is indeed in the bosom of the Sun Râ, in the Solar Barge that the Egyptians located their supreme Paradise.[2]

---

[1] Firmicus says to an Isiac: "Thou shalt not be reclaimed by the splendour of the light shown to thee" (*Nec ostensi tibi luminis splendore corrigeris*). Also in the Mysteries of Eleusis we find this somewhat clap-trap device of an outburst of light in the midst of darkness (*cf.* P. Foucart, *l. l.*, p. 58).

[2] How the Isiacs conceived of Paradise is not yet ascertained. However there is a wish often expressed in their funeral stelæ: "May Osiris grant refreshing water to thy thirsty soul," which

Osiris himself, united with the sun, became one with the star whose daily death and rebirth are another symbol of human destiny. At this stage of the initiation, the neophyte, first identified with Osiris, then with Râ, "was borne through all the elements and approached the gods above and the gods below." So did the blessed Egyptian, who in the other world "adored the morning sun, the moon, the air, the water, and fire."[1] Perhaps the initiate was shown, from the Sacred Books, the journeyings of the Solar Barge; perhaps he was supposed to wander through the twelve Elysian regions that correspond to the twelve hours of the night. This would explain the twelve sacerdotal robes that he puts on during the course of his initiation. We learn from Porphyrius that "the souls in passing through the spheres of the planets put on, like successive tunics, the qualities of those stars."[2] Be that as it may, the neophyte, his initiation over, is supposed to be absorbed into the Sun Râ as was Osiris, as were all the Egyptian

---

certainly is derived from an Egyptian formula: "To drink from the waters of the flowing Nile," one of the joys of the elect in the Egyptian Paradise (cf. Lafaye, l. c., p. 96; Cumont, l. c., p. 437).

[1] Formulæ in the Rhind papyrus (Brugsch, *Die Aegyptologie*, p. 191).

[2] *De abstinentia*, i, 31.

dead;[1] when he reappears before the people, his head is crowned with a halo of rays, like unto the Sun Râ (*ad instar Solis*).

No doubt, after the ecstasy of the sublime revelations, during which he has thrown off his mortal coil, and body of humiliation, the initiate, on his return to his daily human life will find temptations and sorrows awaiting him, and will experience relapses. But he "carries in his soul as in a basket, the pure doctrines" which fortify him against discouragement; he possesses a system of belief, which, as Plutarch puts it, helps him to conform to the laws and to understand the antinomies of our universe. What is Osiris, if not the personification of the good in nature, the supreme intelligence? In a word, Osiris is Good. Seth-Typhon, opposed to him, like drought to moisture, like passion and violence to harmony and justice, is Evil. Between the two, there is an eternal confiiet, played out in the heart of man, but the two are necessary, because each is the complement of the other. Without Evil, Good would not have manifested itself. As for Isis, the feminine

---

[1] To describe the death of Pharaoh, the Egyptian texts say: "The King soars to Heaven and assumes the shape of the solar disc while his limbs are absorbed in the matter of which he was created" (*Louvre Papyrus*, pp. 19, 41, 47).

principle, the universal womb, she is the experimental soil to be fertilised either by Good or Evil. Doubtless, she hates Evil and loves Good with an inherent love, but though she loves, saves, and resuscitates Osiris, she does not kill Typhon, for she knows that it is Evil that has brought about the beneficent death of the "Good Being."[1]   In the Osirian drama, Good is victorious only because Evil has compelled it to assert itself.   Thus man is ever divided between calls, that of his lower instinct, and that of his moral conscience.   Like Osiris, he shall triumph if he has trust in the noble inspirations of Isis.   Then he will understand that "to know the gods by their revelations is to possess the truth," and that "thé most acceptable sacrifice to be offered to the gods is a conscience clear and just, as far from superstition as from atheism."[2]   "To approach nearer and nearer to truth and wisdom," is then, according to Plutarch, what the goddess invites us to seek in ourselves and in her, by the observance of her rites.

But the initiate left the temple with another benefit, more direct and practical, the promise of which Lucius receives from the mouth of the goddess:

[1] *De Iside et Osiride*, 40, 49.          [2] *Ibid.*, I, 2, II.

13

Thou shalt live blessed, thou shalt live crowned with glory beneath my protection, and when thy life is run and thou goest down to the Nether World, there also, in that nether atmosphere, thou shalt see me shining in the inmost halls of Styx; and thou shalt dwell in the Elysian Fields, and continually make offering of worship to me, and I will smile upon thee. Nay, if by sedulous observance and religious service and persistent chastity thou bear thee worthy of my godhead, thou shalt know that I alone have power to prolong thy life beyond the space ordained by fate.[1]

In times past, the Egyptian devotees had aspired to the same bliss: "To come forth after a very happy and prolonged old age among the liegemen of Osiris." But the prospect of a long life on earth became desirable only because the initiate now knew the meaning of this life and no longer feared death. Cicero thus expresses his faith in the Mysteries: "We at last possess reasons why we should live, and we are not only eager to live, but we cherish a better hope in death."[2] The same sentiment is found in the inscription of an Eleusinian initiate: "Behold! it is a fair mystery that comes unto us from the Blessed; for mortals, death is no more an evil, but a

[1] *Metamorphoses*, xi, 6.  H. E. Butler's translation.
[2] Cicero, *De legibus*, ii, 14.

I. High Priest Offering the Holy Water to
the Isiaques.

II. Pantomime in the Isiaque Cult.
(Fresques d'Herculaneum.—E. Guimet, *L'Isis
romaine*).

Plate XVI.

bliss."[1] This peace of the soul, the supreme boon of the Isiac initiation, is also expressed in a phrase often found on the tombs of the initiated: "Have faith in Osiris!"

Despite its shortcomings and some obscurity in its symbols, the worship of Isis succeeded in holding its ground in the Roman world for a period of five hundred years. The Christian faith, in its infancy, had no better equipped rival. "The whole world now swears by Serapis," exclaimed Tertullian indignantly. In fact, with its priesthood, white-robed, tonsured, of ascetic life; its congregation of believers, its monks and nuns; its ceremonies of baptism and communion; its doctrines of salvation and redemption; its preachings from the pulpit, its daily services in the temple; its habits of contemplation and ecstatic adoration; its yearning for truth and justice,—the cult of Isis appears as a sort of pre-Christianity. On certain points, the resemblance was such indeed that the

[1] Plutarch (*Immortality of the Soul*) says: "Then the initiate, made perfect and free, walks without constraint and celebrates the Mysteries with a crown on his head. He lives with men who are pure and sanctified; he looks beneath him upon the earth, upon the crowd of the folk who are not initiated and purified and who throng to the mud-pit and flounder in the darkness, and through fear of death cling to their woes, not trusting in the bliss of the hereafter."

Fathers regarded it as a kind of parody: "May not the devil in the mysteries of the idols counterfeit things of our divine faith? He also baptises those who believe in him, and promises that they shall come forth, cleansed of their sins."[1]

At any rate, it is through the channel of the Mystéries of Isis that the speculations of Ancient Egypt have spread over the Roman world, but the evolution from Egyptian thought to Isiac doctrines marks a progress. At 'the beginning, the sacrifice of the god in Egypt was involuntary and its redemptory effects upon mankind were unconscious. It is the force of a purely magic rite that resuscitates Osiris, and it is as a consequence of a magic axiom, "Like produces like," that the men who imitate the death of Osiris partake automatically in his rebirth and immortality. As we advance in Egyptian civilisation, the sacrifice of the god develops more and more into a self-conscious act, in the supreme altruism of the "Good Being."[2] At the epoch of the Mysteries of Isis, the evolution in the spiritualistic direction is quite completed; it is Isis herself who calls the neophyte (Lucius styles himself *vocatus*), who entreats him to follow the way of Osiris, who leads him on the road to salvation. The Isiac baptism

---

[1] Tertullian, *De præsc. hæreticorum*, xli.     [2] See *ante*, p. 98.

is for the cleansing of the soul rather than of the body; the death of the neophyte typifies the death of the soul unto sin; the rebirth is the starting-point for a purer and higher life; the outburst of light in the darkness symbolises the illumination of the mind by the revealed truths; the transfiguration of the initiate into the god Râ is the apotheosis of man, who knowing God, himself becomes divine.

The Isiac creed appealed forcibly to men by its direct call to the individual. The Roman religion, cold and formal, a State sacerdotal office, associating man with God only through the intermediary of the priest, had failed to touch the hearts, stir imagination, or move the depths of enthusiasm. The votary of Isis, wrapt in ecstasy at the feet of the goddess, interpreted the revelation not in the word, but in the spirit, according to the need of his heart, in the glow of his faith. From that day Mysticism has lived. The Isiac became his own priest; the god, no longer a far-distant entity, a remote State providence, deigns to converse with him, becomes his tutelary friend, and, as it were, "a thing of beauty and a joy for ever." Each man "possesses" the God who is father of all, and keeps his law in doing good in his own way.

These Isiac mystics are at the same time ascetics. To know God, man must live soberly, chastely, and die to the things of this world. Greek philosophy, on the contrary, taught man "to live his life" (*carpe diem*), and to seek the supreme good on this earth by the light of reason, wisdom, righteousness. The Oriental mysteries may also have conferred upon Cicero and other initiates an eagerness to live to relish all the joys of life. Isis promises to Lucius that he shall enjoy a lengthy earthly happiness. But supreme happiness is a boon of the next world; it is the hope held out to the initiated, as, later, to the Christians. By the influence of Eastern religions, a new character is imparted to the aspirations of men. Life is desirable, yet, in the confines of this perishable body, it is only a preparation, a stage upon the road to death.[1] Man has vanquished for ever his terror of the unknown. One step further, and he will despise all earthly joys, his eyes fixed upon the vision of eternal bliss promised by Christ!

[1] *Cf*. Plutarch, *De Iside et Osiride*, 2. "Isis communicates her holy creed to those who by their perseverance in a temperate life, withdrawing themselves from the pleasures of the senses and from the passions, yearn to participate in the divine nature; who observe sedulously in the temples severe rules and rigorous abstinence, that they may know the Supreme and Sovereign Being whom the Spirit alone can understand, whom the goddess invites us to seek in herself, as in the sanctuary where he abides."

# CHAPTER VI

## Some Legendary Travels of the Egyptians in Asia

BEYOND the State documents, accounts of campaigns, annals of the reigns of the Pharaohs, lists of conquests, and treaties of peace, which afford us, if not an insight, at least a glimpse into the history of the political and military intercourse between Egypt and Asia, we possess other Egyptian material. It consists of legends and anecdotes of a purely imaginative character, unreliable for the historian, but valuable in that it reveals how the Egyptians pictured to themselves the regions of Asia bordering their own country. These texts take the form of biographical inscriptions, popular tales, and rhetorical exercises, and do not claim to give any accurate information concerning chronology, or geography. But to him who wishes to know the life and primitive customs of the countries explored by the Egyptians, as well as the point of view taken by the Egyptian explorer, even such descriptions, fantastic though they be, will afford a few precious guides and provide a pleasing relief to the bare statements of official history.

The oldest account of this kind with which we are acquainted is entitled *The Adventures of Sinouhit*. [1]

About 2000 B.C., during the reign of Amenemhait I, a great Egyptian lord left the court secretly, for reasons that are not made clear, and took refuge beyond the Asiatic frontier in a country called Kedem, situated in the Upper Tonou. There, Sinouhit was heartily welcomed by the Prince of Tonou, Ammouianashi, who said to him, "Thou shalt feel at home in my land, for thou wilt hear the speech of Egypt." Not that the country was colonised by Egyptians, but it gave shelter to a certain number of refugees, like Sinouhit himself. The interest of the story for us lies in the description given by the Egyptian nobleman of the country in which he settled, and of its customs.

The Lord of Tonou gave me his eldest daughter in marriage and he granted that I should choose for myself, in his country, a portion from the best land he possessed on the frontier of a neighbouring state.

[1] Berlin Papyrus, No 1.

The land is excellent; Asia is its name. Figs and grapes grow therein; wine is more abundant than water; there is honey in plenty, oil in great quantity, and all kinds of fruit are on the trees; barley and wheat grow there beyond measure, and there is every kind of cattle. And the prince of the land honoured me, making me a prince over one of the best tribes in his dominions. I had bread for every meal and wine every day, boiled meat and roasted poultry, also the game that was caught for me or presented to me, besides that which was chased by my own hounds. Dishes in plenty were prepared for me and I had milk cooked in all sorts of ways.

I passed many years there; my children became mighty, each one lord of his own tribe. The messenger who went down to the north or who came up to the south toward Egypt was eager to visit me, for I welcomed everybody. . . . The Bedouins (*Satiou*), who set out upon far-off expeditions to fight and to conquer the alien princes, were under my command, for the prince of Tonou appointed me general of his soldiers for many years. . . .

A mighty man of Tonou came to defy me in my tent; . . . he declared that he would seize my cattle at the instigation of his tribe. . . . I spent the night in stringing my bow, arranging my arrows, sharpening my sword, and furbishing my weapons. At daybreak, all the people of Tonou thronged around me; . . . all hearts burned for me, men and women uttered cries, every heart was fearful for me, and they said, "Is there verily another mighty man who dare fight against him?" He took his shield, his battle-axe, his armful of javelins. When I had made him use all his spears and had dodged his arrows so that they struck

the earth far and wide, he rushed upon me; then I
drew my bow upon him, and when my arrow entered
his neck, he uttered a great cry and he fell upon the
ground. I despatched him with his own axe. I stood
upon his back and sent up my cry of victory and all
the Asiatics shouted for joy . . . and the prince
Ammouianashi embraced me, and I seized the
possessions of the slain. . . .[1]

The remainder of the story is not concerned
with Asia. Sinouhit, reinstated in the favour
of Pharaoh, returns to Egypt. His vivid descriptions of the pastoral and warlike life of the people
of Tonou,[2] of the political organisation of the land
under the rule of petty chieftains of clans owing
allegiance to a paramount chief, would have a still
greater interest for us, if we could only locate the
district with accuracy. We find applied to those
localities, names, which in the Bible, designate men;
thus, the Ajah of Genesis,[3] a nephew of Lotan.[4]

The name Tonou, according to Max Müller, R.
Weill, and Isidore Lévy,[5] would be an abbreviated
form of Lotan, Lotanou. The region here described would therefore be the land stretching

[1] Trans.: G. Maspero, _Les Contes populaires de l'Égypte
ancienne._

[2] The land of Tonou is in later documents called by the Egyptians Retonou, Lotenou, Lotanou.          [3] Genesis xxxvi, 24.

[4] Genesis xxxvi, 20. G. Maspero, _Les Mémoires de Sinouhit,_
1908, p. 45.

[5] _Sphinx_, t. viii, p. 214; t. ix, pp. 10, 72.

between the Dead Sea and the Desert of Sinai, a view that seems to be supported by a statement on an official stela in Sinai, dated from Amenemhait III, which refers to a connection between Egypt and the brother of a chieftain of Lotanou.[1]

But a recent discovery has challenged this identification. In a bundle of papyri found by M. Quibell in the Ramesseum, there has come to light another manuscript of our story, and Mr. Alan H. Gardiner has established the reading in it of a very important name, illegible in the Berlin papyrus; this is the name of *Kepni-Gebli-Gebel*, which is another name for Byblos on the Syrian coast.[2]    Hence, it is around Byblos that the scenes of pastoral life, described by Sinouhit, should be placed.    If that is so, we must conclude according to Gardiner, that Palestine, at the time of the XIIth dynasty was still undeveloped, since the mainland away from the coast had no towns and the inhabitants still led a pastoral and nomadic life. Hence arises another objection.    According to the chronology adopted by the Berlin school, the XIIth Egyptian dynasty would be separated from the XVIIIth by an interval of only two hundred years.

[1] R. Weill, ap. *Sphinx*, t. ix, pp. 9, 67.

[2] Alan H. Gardiner, *Eine neue Handschrift der Sinuhegeschichte* (Ber. Berlin. Akad., 7 Feb., 1907).

But during the XVIIIth dynasty (about 1600 B.C.,) as is clearly evidenced by the letters found at El-Amarna,[1] there existed in Palestine a municipal system of government. Such an evolution and total change of policy could hardly have been brought about and developed in the short space of two centuries.

I cannot enter here upon the discussion of all the various problems put forward by the adventures of Sinouhit. Let it be briefly added that in a recent edition of the text, Maspero disputes the reading of *Kepni* and returns to his previous conclusions in favour of a country near Sinai.[2]

Yet it must be pointed out that the Egyptians, at the time of Amenemhait I were perfectly familiar with Byblos, for it appears from a recent discovery that mention was made of an Egyptian expedition to Byblos,[3] under the Ancient Empire, that is, centuries before the time when Sinouhit set out upon his adventurous journey.

---

[1] A. Moret, *In the Time of the Pharaohs*, Ch. II: Pharaonic Diplomacy.

[2] R. Weill suggests that *Kepni, Gebel*, retains here its wide geographical meaning, "the mountains" (*Sphinx*, xi, p. 204). Gardiner holds his own ground (*Die Erzählung des Sinuhe*, 1909, p. 10), supported by Ed. Meyer (*Geschichte*, i, 2d ed., p. 396).

[3] Sethe et Gardiner, ap. *Zeitschift für ægyptische Sprache*, xlv, p. 10. For mention of Byblos in the Egyptian texts of the XIIth dynasty, see Erman, *A. Z.*, xlii, p. 60.

After Thotmes I, about 1550 B.C., had conquered·
Syria, the valley of the Jordan, and the land
beyond as far as the banks of the Euphrates, the
Egyptians held sway, for many centuries, over
these regions of Lotanou and Kharou.   But their
curiosity and interest seem to have carried them
to still more distant lands which made an appeal
to their imaginations.   The spectacle of the Euphrates astonishes them.   "Its waters turned back
go down-stream in going up-stream," says Thotmes I, in the stela of Tombos.[1]   They speak with
awe of the forests of Lebanon where the noble
Sennofri, a favourite of Thotmes III, pitched his
tent at an altitude that seemed fabulous to the inhabitants of the Nile valley—"above the clouds";
penetrated into the forest and brought back to
Byblos choice trunks of the cedar-trees, sixty
Egyptian cubits (about 34 yards) in length, and as
thick at one end as at the other.   At Byblos, the
cedars were packed upon ships and sent down into
Egypt.   The conquerors of these far-off provinces
seize the opportunity to relate to us their own
achievements in the chase and in warfare.   Amenemheb, one of the officers of Thotmes III has

[1] Stele of Tombos, l. 13 (Lepsius, *Denkmäler*, iii, 5, *a*).   For
the Egyptian on the Nile, north was down-stream, and south
up-stream.   Hence their surprise when they saw that on the
Euphrates one went south in going down-stream.

engraved his exploits on the walls of his tomb. In the country of Nii, he "slew one hundred and twenty elephants in order to take their tusks." "The largest of the elephants had charged His Majesty; I cut off his trunk [literally his hand] while he stood alive before His Majesty." At the siege of Qadesh, the enemy sent a mare in rut amongst the stallions of the Egyptian chariots, to disarray their ranks. Amenemheb sprang from his chariot, rushed upon the mare, ripped her up with his sword, cut off her tail, and brought it back to the King as a trophy. Such feats won their reward. The son of Thotmes III, Amenophis II, one day, while holding a review, called Amenemheb from the ranks: "I know thy courage," he said to him; "thou shalt have the command of my chosen troops."

Such picturesque material as warlike deeds, hunting exploits, wild country, dark forests, was likely to appeal to the popular imagination. A mass of legend was built up at that time, but few of the many tales have come down to us. They have all the same adventurous character and relate at length the heroic doings of the Egyptians in Asia, but say very little concerning the country itself and the inhabitants thereof—the very points on which we desire information. We hear, for example, how, in the time of Thotmes III, a certain Thoutii, general of the infantry, captured, by stratagem, a rebel chief of Jaffa and felled him with the great staff of Pharaoh;[1] the account may have been gratifying—to the Egyptians—but we would like to learn a little more about Jaffa and the surrounding country.   The story does contain a morsel of historical information, but when we come to the tale of the "Predestined Prince," we are in the heart of the land of fable.

In the land of Naharaina, the region of the upper Euphrates, there is a mysterious town, where in a palace, pierced with seventy windows, rising seventy cubits above the earth, the prince's daughter is hidden away.   He alone will be her husband who can fly from the ground and reach her.   It is the son of Pharaoh, the predestined Prince, who at one bound reaches the window and falls into the arms of the enamoured princess, to the great chagrin of the Syrian princes who have tried in vain daily to wing their flight thus high.[2]

Again, we enter further into the realm of the fantastic in the story of the *Princess of Bakhtan.* We are still in Naharaina.   The prince of Bakhtan,

[1] Maspero's *Popular Tales*, 3d ed., p. 92.
[2] *Harris Papyrus*, 500.

who has given his eldest daughter in marriage to the Pharaoh, beseeches the aid of his mighty son-in-law and ally to release his second daughter, who resides with him, from the possession of an evil spirit. Pharaoh sends magicians, who prove of no avail. Thereupon, he dispatches from Thebes, a statue of the god Khonsu. The god performs a few magnetic passes and forthwith the evil spirit comes out of the princess and departs after it has been granted honourable terms of capitulation.[1] Here, everything is legendary; the subject-matter of the tale, the locality, and the personality of the Pharaoh and of the prince.

Among all these accounts of imaginary travels in Asia, one alone has any resemblance to a geographical romance. It has been translated by Chabas under the title of *The Travels of an Egyptian.*[2] Unfortunately, its text is very fragmentary and difficult to understand. Its hero seems to have been one of those Egyptian messengers, the character and rôle of whom have been quite clearly designed for us in the letters from El-Amarna; they journeyed from town to town as mediators, as protectors, sometimes as judges, in order to enforce the authority of the Pharaoh in the distant

[1] *Stèle* in the Paris National Library.
[2] *Papyrus Anastasi* I.

parts of his dominions.¹ The writer of the story
employs a literary artifice, which is not without its
parallels in our own day. He, himself, addresses
the hero as if recalling to him the travels and
events that have been experienced by him. The
writer emphasises the dangers which faced his
hero in the forests, on the mountainous shores
and the deserts which lay between the towns; he
mentions Byblos, the city of the goddess; Tyre,
where fish are greater in number than the grains of
sand and where drinking-water has to be brought
by boat from the main land. The most fully-
described episode is that of the arrival of the
messenger at Jaffa, by land, through a defile of the
mountains of the Levant:

> Thou goest alone, without any escort in thy train,
> and thou findest no mountaineer to put thee in the
> way thou shouldest go; so terror lays hold upon thee,
> thy hair rises on thy head, thy soul sinks into thy
> sandals, for thy way is blocked by rocks and boulders;
> there is no beaten track; hollies, thorns, aloes, dog-
> shoes (prickly plants?), obstruct thy path; on one side
> rises the precipice, on the other sinks the abyss.
> Whilst thou travellest along, thy chariot jolts un-
> ceasingly, thy team starts at every turn. At last,
> wearied at heart, thou startest to gallop, but the sky
> is cloudless; thou art thirsty, the enemy is behind

¹ See A. Moret, *In the Time of the Pharaohs*, Ch. II: Pharaonic
Diplomacy.

14

thee, thou art affrighted, and when the bough of an acacia lashes thee, thou dost dart aside, thy horse is wounded, thou art thrown to the ground, and thou art bruised.

But on entering Jaffa, thou comest to an orchard in the full season of blossoming, thou makest a hole in the hedge, thou goest in and thou dost eat; thou findest there a fair maiden who keeps the orchards; she makes friends with thee and gives thee the flower of her breast. Thou art discovered, thou announcest who thou art, and every one agrees that thou art a hero!

In brief, the travel tales, written during the dynasty of the Ramses about 1300 B.C., picture for us an imaginary Asia, vague, lacking local colour, serving only as a setting for warlike adventures or amorous enterprises. The description of the customs or of the country is not a matter of interest either for the writer or for the Egyptian reader. The aim of the story is the gratification of national pride in the celebration of the achievements of Pharaoh's subjects.

The special literature of which we are treating did not come to an end after the fall of the Egyptian protectorate in Asia Minor. We have a papyrus, in the Golenischeff collection, describing the travels of an Egyptian in Phœnicia about the eleventh century B.C. As may be expected, the tone of the narrative and the bearing of the Egypt-

ian personages have greatly changed; we feel we
are in a time when the Pharaonic domination is
weakened and disputed.    The hero is no longer a
predestined prince, or a captive princess, or a
powerful magician, or a valorous captain, or a
boastful messenger; he whom we meet in this last
document, hitherto unknown to us, is a simple
clerk engaged in business.

His name is Unamonu and he is a chief-keeper of
the hypostyle hall at Karnak.    In the year 5 of
the reign of Ramses XII, about 1100 B.C., last of the
Ramses, when the high-priest of Amon, Herihor,
had seized the sceptre in the Thebaid, and Smendes, the first king of the Tanite dynasty, ruled the
Delta at Tanis, Unamonu embarked upon the
Syrian Seas to find wood to build a bark for Amon-
Râ.    He touched at Dor, the city of the Zakkalas,
north of Jaffa, then at Tyre, and at Byblos, arriving
eventually in the country of Alasia, a land not yet
identified, though some recognise it as Cyprus,
while others place it at the mouth of the Orontes.

The voyage is full of events.    Unamonu had
manned his ship with Syrians.    At the port of Dor,
one of his sailors runs away, taking with him vases
and ingots of gold and silver, intended for the
princes ruling along the coast.    He cannot obtain
justice either at Dor, or at Tyre, and when he

arrives at Byblos, and the Prince Zerkarbaal hears that he has brought no presents, an order is issued that he must leave the port. But the gods immediately express their displeasure. As the Prince of Byblos was sacrificing in the temple, the gods seized one of the favourite courtiers and made him dance till he fell into a condition of frenzy and prophecy that lasted all day and all night. The Egyptian was called úpon to deliver him from this possession and came, bringing with him a statue of Amon, reserved for foreign expeditions and therefore called "Amon of the Ways." The statue probably played the same part as the statue of Khonsu in the tale of the Princess of Bakhtan; the magic intervention was successful, then they turned to business.

Unamonu was led to the palace and found the Prince "seated in his chamber on high, leaning his back against a balcony while the waves of the great Syrian sea broke behind him." The Prince declared he would not grant any loads of timber unless the Egyptian brought him, according to the old custom, presents of equal value.

"In times past," he said, "my fathers executed the wishes of the Pharaohs, because Pharaoh was wont to send six vessels laden with the merchandise of Egypt to be unloaded in our docks. Thou, then,

cause the same to be brought also unto me!" He
had the account books of his father brought to him
and he had them read in my presence, and it was
found that in all, one thousand *tabonou* of silver (two
hundred pounds) were entered in his books. And
he said to me: "If the king of Egypt were my master, and I, even I, were his servant, he would not
have to cause gold and silver to be brought here,
saying: Perform the mission of Amon. It was not a
royal command that was brought to my father. And
I, verily I, I am not, even I, thy servant; I am not, I,
the servant of him who hath sent thee."

To these insolent speeches, Unamonu retorts in
no less high-sounding language, but he agrees to
despatch into Egypt a messenger on a ship convey-
ing seven loads of timber, and some weeks later,
the messenger returns with presents sent by King
Smendes of Tanis. There were four jugs and a
basin of gold, five jugs of silver, ten pieces of royal
linen, five hundred rolls of fine papyrus, five hundred ox-hides, five hundred cables, sacks of lentils,
and dried fish. The present was of sufficient value,
for the Prince of Byblos "levied three hundred
men, with three hundred oxen, and put overseers
at their head, for the felling of the trees; the timber
remained all winter lying on the ground; then in the
third month of the harvest-time, it was hauled
down to the shore."

The Egyptian messenger is about to set sail when a new delay is enforced upon him, the Prince of Byblos invites him, ironically, to visit the tombs in which are laid the remains of the messengers of Pharaoh Khamois (probably Ramses XI); they had come hither on a similar mission, but were detained for seventeen years in Byblos and had never returned to Egypt.   This last insult plunges Unamonu into the deepest despair, the more so as he sees looming on the horizon of the sea eleven ships of the Zakkalas, hostile pirates, ready to capture him as soon as he leaves port.   Then, said the messenger, "I sat down and wept; the scribe of the Prince came out to me and said to me, 'What ails thee?' I replied, 'Seest thou not the birds (the herons?) who return into Egypt? Behold! they fly back to their cool waters, but I, how long shall I stay here, abandoned?' "[1]   The Prince, on hearing this, sent the Egyptian two vessels of wine, a sheep, and Tantnouit, a song-stress from Egypt, who lived in the palace, saying: "Sing to him, let not his heart be filled with sad thoughts!"   And he sent a message to the Zak-kalas: "I cannot take prisoner the messenger

---

[1] This theme was employed by Flaubert in an admirable passage of Salambo, where she laments at the sight of the doves of Carthage flying towards Italy.

of Amon in my own country. Give him a chance
to depart, and then you run after him and capture
him."

On leaving Byblos, the wind casts Unamonu on
the shores of Alasia. But here the papyrus breaks
off, at the very moment when the messenger is relating his misfortunes to Hataba the queen of the
country, and trying to move her heart on his behalf.

The historical interest of this tale must be
obvious to every reader. It throws a faint but
valuable light upon one of the most obscure points
in the history—as far as yet known—of the intercourse between Egypt and Asia. It refers to the
population of the Zakkalas, who with the Philis-
tines and others (the Shagalashas and Uashashas)
were subjugated by Ramses III, conqueror of the
peoples of the sea; he rid himself of the Zakkalas
by assigning to them the coast between Carmel and
Egypt. Now we see them, settled at Dor, roving
the seas in their pirate ships and raiding trading-
vessels. As for the Phœnicians, settled between
Tyre and Byblos, the insolent words of the Prince
of Byblos sufficiently express their new position
towards Egypt. Doubtless, Egypt still enjoys
amongst these strange people, a certain prestige,
resting upon the long-revered name of the Pharaohs, upon her mighty gods, upon her great wealth,

but her force of conquest is exhausted; her emissaries are no longer feared, since certain of them remained for seventeen years in Byblos and died in bondage there; again, if the chieftains of Lebanon still permit their timber to be exported to Egypt for building purposes, it is only upon immediate payment.    Egypt is in her decline.

To sum up, if this legendary literature affords very little information regarding the political relations of Egypt with Asia, it throws some new light upon the Egyptian character.   The Egyptians do not appear to have brought to their observation of foreign people any great faculty, either of curiosity or of admiration.   But neither do they seem to have felt for them the customary disdain of the civilised man for the barbarian.   What chiefly interested them outside Egypt, was still the Egyptians.   Moreover, their intimate knowledge of strange lands was confined to the regions about the Nile.   None ventured beyond Lebanon, save a few soldiers, or emissaries and travellers by profession.   For the common folk, these far-off lands were fraught with danger, mystery.   Such a mental attitude is likely to foster the growth of popular romances, but hardly lends itself to the production of documents valuable to the historian.

# CHAPTER VII

## HOMER AND EGYPT

THE importance of Oriental influences upon the early development of Hellenic civilisation is no longer disputed; rather, it is a fact widely recognised. Limiting our subject to the Homeric poems, the investigations by scholars like Helbig, Victor Bérard, and Murray, of the material of the *Iliad* and the *Odyssey*, have led to the discovery of many an Oriental tradition, especially in the poetic and artistic treatment of certain passages.

But if the truth of this assertion is broadly admitted as a general principle, it has not yet been followed up and verified in all its particular applications. Hence it may be of interest to point out a few passages in the *Iliad* and the *Odyssey*, in which the Homeric Bards seem to have drawn freely upon the art and popular literature of Egypt.

An examination of the subject must be a purely

academic study. In order to prove that here or there "Homer borrows from Egypt," I cannot speculate with general ideas nor make a call upon our imaginative faculties; I am compelled to go into the most petty, tedious details. I must therefore ask the reader to bear patiently with a demonstration which cannot avoid the barren aspect of a piece of research work.

In his remarkable book on the *Phœnicians and the Odyssey*,[1] V. Bérard affirms, by the aid of ingenious arguments, that the episode of the sojourn of Menelaus in Egypt "was but the Greek adaptation of an Egyptian tale." Menelaus, held back by the gods in the island of Pharos, near to Egypt, only succeeds in appeasing their anger, when he has overcome, by stratagem, the Egyptian Proteus, the Old Man of the Sea. This skilled magician knows the depths of all the seas, and can transform himself, according to the danger that menaces him, into a lion, a dragon, a panther, a boar; into water, fire, or a tree. But Menelaus succeeds in seizing him and compels him to reveal the way of escape from Egypt, the fate of his companions on leaving Troy, and the fate in store for him. Thus spake Proteus:

[1] ii, p. 65 *et seq.*

But thou, Menelaus, son of Zeus, art not ordained to die and meet thy fate in Argos, the pasture-land of horses, but the deathless gods will convey thee to the Elysian plain and the world's end, where is Rhadamanthus of the fair hair, where life is easiest for men. No snow is there, nor yet great storm, nor any rain; but always ocean sendeth forth the breeze of the shrill West to blow cool on men. [1]

This legend bears a clear Egyptian imprint. The Proteus of Homer, like the Proteus of Herodotus and Virgil, [2] is, as V. Bérard has pointed out, the Egyptian *Prouti*, the Pharaoh, son of the gods, expert magician, who can, like all Egyptian sorcerers, suspend the flow of the rivers and of the waters of the sea, overthrow earth and heaven, and assume any form he likes. As for the isle of Pharos, would it not be "the Isle of Pharaoh"? In any case, the Elysian Fields take the form of a landscape of Egypt, the land that knows neither rain nor snow. There reigns, as in the Egyptian Fields of Ialou, Osiris, lord of Amenti, under the name of Rhadamanthus; there, blows the Zephyr, the cold wind of the North-West, so dreaded by the Greeks, since it brought rain and gales, so welcome to the Egyptians, to whom it brought pleasant refreshment, as it does even to-day after the sultry

---

[1] *Odyssey*, iv, 560–567. Tr.: Butcher and Lang.
[2] Herodotus, ii, 112–116. Virgil, *Georgics*, iv, 364 *et seq.*

tempests of the April Khamsin, or the tropical heat of summer days. On the ancient funeral stelæ the desire is constantly expressed by the dead that he may "breathe the gentle wind of the North." In a hot country, like Egypt, what wonder that his conception of Paradise was a land of pleasant coolness? Thence, also, his wish to "drink of the flowing waters of the river." Later, we see the Isiacs pray to Osiris to grant them "cool water." From them, the prayer passed on to the Romans, who termed the Paradise where the dead shall find coolness and bliss, *refrigerium*. Finally, the very same expression finds a place in the Christian liturgy, where we pray for the spiritual "refreshment" of our dead, though the Christian Paradise of to-day retains little resemlance to the Fields of Ialou. The Paradisiac ideal of Homer is certainly foreign in its conception, and all its features point to an Egyptian source. It is, therefore, very probable that the *Nostos* of Menelaus is imitated from an Egyptian tale.

But if this *Nostos* contains topics commonplace in Egyptian folk-lore, it refers to no particular narrative. On the contrary, a strict parallelism is now possible between an episode in the *Odyssey*—

the Shipwreck of Ulysses in the land of the Phæacians—and an Egyptian tale; for there has recently
come to light an hieratic papyrus of the XIIth
dynasty, which has been published, translated,
and commented upon by M. W. Golenischeff.[1]
Both relate the adventures of a seafaring man,
who having set sail in fair weather is suddenly
overtaken by a storm. Let us hear the Egyptian
tale first:

I went down to the sea in a ship one hundred and
fifty cubits long, forty cubits broad, with one hundred
and fifty sailors, the best in Egypt, who had seen the
sky and the earth, and whose hearts were bolder than
lions; they could predict a storm before it came, and a
tempest before it arose. [Nevertheless] the storm
came, suddenly, when we were out at sea. We made
for the land; the wind carried us thither, and caused
the waves to increase and rise to a height of eight
cubits. A plank of wood was afloat. I seized upon it.
As for the ship! all who remained upon her were
drowned, none excepted. And lo! I was washed upon
an island by a wave of the sea. I passed three days
(there) alone, with (only) my heart for a companion.
I slept in a wood that formed a hiding-place, where the
shadows covered me. Then I stretched out my legs,
went to find something to put in my mouth. I found
there, figs, grapes, all kinds of magnificent leeks,

[1] W. Golenischeff, *Papyrus 115 of the Imperial Hermitage, St.
Petersburg* (ap. *Recueil de travaux relatifs à la philologie égyptienne*,
xxviii, pp. 73–112). I follow in the main Golenischeff's translation, but endeavour to keep more closely to the text.

berries, seeds, melons plentiful as dust of the earth, fish, and birds; there was nothing that was not there. So I ate my fill, then I placed on the earth a portion of the abundance that filled my hands. I dug a pit, I made a fire, I raised a pile that (the offerings) might pass by the fire to the gods.

Let us turn to Odysseus. He embarked alone for Calypso's island; after sailing for eighteen days without any incident occurring, there loomed before him "the shadowy hills of the land of the Phæacians." But Zeus lets loose a storm and a great wave "smites down upon him" and shatters his raft to pieces. Odysseus "bestrides a single beam as one rideth a courser."[1] For three days and three nights he keeps afloat and "ponders in his heart."[2] Finally "a great wave bears him to the rugged shore."[3] He takes shelter in a wood; he creeps between "twin bushes secluded from wind, rain, and sun," and he falls asleep.[4] In another passage he describes the wonderful vegetation of the blessed land of the Phæacians: "There grew tall trees blossoming, pear-trees and pomegranates, apple-trees with bright fruit, and sweet figs and olives in their bloom, . . . and cluster upon cluster of the grape."[5] There is no

[1] *Od.*, v, 365 *et seq.*    [2] *Od.*, v, 424.    [3] *Od.*, v, 425.
[4] *Od.*, v, 475–493.    [5] *Od.*, vii, 114 *et seq.*

mention here of offerings to the gods of the country, but as M. Golenischeff points out, it occurs in the episode of Odysseus and Polyphemus. There, arrived at the cave of Cyclops, Odysseus and his companions "kindled a fire and made burnt offerings . . . and took of the cheeses and did eat."[1]

Listen again to the words of the shipwrecked Egyptian:

And lo! I heard a voice of thunder. I uncovered my face and I saw a great serpent approaching. . . . He said to me: "Who has brought thee hither, little one? who has brought thee hither? . . ." Then he took me in his mouth and he carried me over to the place where he stayed. . . . And he said to me (again): "Who has brought thee, little one, who has brought thee to this island of the sea, where the two shores are in the waters?"

Thereupon, the Shipwrecked Mariner replies to him in the story related above.

As for Odysseus, he is welcomed in Phæacia by Nausicaa, by King Alcinous and his subjects— that is, by human beings, not by monsters. Therefore, no sound like thunder announces the arrival of the Phæacians. In the episode of Polyphemus, on the contrary, the Cyclops enters with a great

[1] *Od.*, ix, 231.

din[1] into the cave in which Odysseus has taken refuge. M. Golenischeff remarks upon a striking detail; when the Egyptian awakens, he "uncovers" his face that he may see; so also the companions of Odysseus, asleep on the beach, when they are awakened by the voice of their master.[2] Gesture and attitude are again similar when the serpent lifts up the Shipwrecked Mariner from the side of his burnt offering and transports him to his own seat;[3] and when Alcinous, finding his guest "sitting near the ashes" of the hearth, takes him by the hand, raises him, and leads him to a shining chair. Again, in the episode of the Phæacians, as in the papyrus, the hero has to answer twice the same questions. First, Queen Arete asks him, "Who art thou?"[4] Later, Alcinous repeats the questions[5] and, like the Shipwrecked Mariner, Odysseus gives an account of his misfortunes.

In his reply to the Shipwrecked Mariner, the Serpent shows himself benevolent and kindly.

Fear nothing, fear nothing, little one, let not thy countenance be sad. Thou hast come unto me because God has granted that thou shouldst live, and he has led thee to this enchanted island. . . . Behold! thou shalt pass here month after month,

[1] *Od.*, ix, 235.    [2] *Od.*, x, 179.    [3] *Od.*, vii, 168.
[4] *Od.*, vii, 237.              [5] *Od.*, viii, 548.

until it comes to pass that thou hast spent four months in this island; and a vessel shall come from the country [literally, from the Court] with sailors, whom thou hast known; thou shalt depart with them for thy country and thou shalt die in thine own city. . . . Thou shalt press thy children to thy bosom, thou shalt embrace thy wife, thou shalt behold thy home, which is better than all; thou shalt reach thy own land and thou shalt live there among thy brothers. . . .

Similar words welcome Odysseus among the Phæacians. Nausicaa says to him: "It is Zeus who giveth weal to men, and thy lot is of him and so thou must endure it. . . ."[1] For the poor and strangers are near the heart of Zeus. That is why Zeus, like the Egyptian god, foretells the return of Odysseus,[2] who yearns to see again "his noble wife in his home, and his friends unharmed."[3] Nausicaa and Alcinous, in turn, wish him the experience of this joy in his native land.

The gratitude of the Shipwrecked Mariner manifests itself in rapturous promises: "I will describe thy souls to Pharaoh; I will make known to him thy greatness; I will send to thee holy oils and incense[4] such as are offered to the gods; I will

---

[1] *Od.*, vi, 189.    [2] *Od.*, xiii, 133.    [3] *Od.*, xiii, 42-43.

[4] In a passage non-essential for comparison with the Homeric text, the Serpent answers ironically: "Thou art not rich in perfumes *ânti*, for all thou hast is but incense (*sonter nouter*); but I who am the Lord of the land of Punt, I have there the perfume

send to thee ships full of the treasures of Egypt, as is fitting for a god. . . ." In the same way, when Odysseus thanks Alcinous, he prophesies for him glory imperishable by the side of Zeus,[1] and to Nausicaa, he says that he will "worship her as though she were a god."[2]

The Serpent, replying to the compliments of the Shipwrecked Mariner, says: "I am the lord of the Land of Punt . . . and lo! it shall happen that as soon as thou art departed from this place, thou shalt never behold it more, for it shall be transformed into waters." And to add to the fantastic character of the island, the Shipwrecked Mariner remarks that "it was a distant country that no man knew." Likewise, the Phæacians

---

*ânti.* . . ." M. Golenischeff adds an apt remark about the serpent form of the lord of the Land of Spices and Perfumes. Our tale re-echoes ancient fables concerning the inhabitants of countries like Punt, or concerning the Egyptian dealers along the Red Sea; they tried to conceal the origin of the scented gums and other perfumes, and emphasised the dangers encountering the seekers of these substances. This was that they might demand high prices for them. Herodotus tells us that the Arabs who gather incense "must drive away a multitude of little flying serpents who guard the trees." Theophrastus also tells us that one gathers cinnamon after "driving away many serpents, the bite of which is deadly" (*Hist. plant.*, ix, 5). On certain coasts of Arabia, incense belonged exclusively to the king of the country (see *Périple de la mer Érythrée*, 12); this explains why the king of the island appears under the guise of a great reptile, surrounded by a family of seventy-five serpents.

[1] *Od.*, vii, 333.          [2] *Od.*, viii, 467. *Cf.* vi, 8.

are said to inhabit the island of Scheria, "far from civilised man"; according to the words of Nausicaa: "Far apart we live, in the wash of the waves, the outermost of men, and no other mortals are conversant with us."[1] Here M. Golenischeff remarks again: "The fact that the Serpent-King 'prince of Punt' is supposed to be living with all his family, not in his own kingdom, but upon an island, is in keeping with the Homeric statement that the Phæacians also were dwelling upon an island, Scheria, instead of in their own country of Hyperia,[2] whence they fled because the Cyclopes 'harried them continually, being mightier than they.'" Finally, like the island of our papyrus that shall disappear beneath the waves after the departure of the Shipwrecked Mariner, so the island of Scheria is doomed to destruction after Odysseus has left it. Poseidon, who hates the Phæacians, "will overshadow their city with a huge mountain."[3] In either case, it is the king of the island who divulges the fate of the island to the hero of the tale.

At the moment when the farewells are uttered, the Serpent renews his good wishes: "Good health, good health, little one, even to thy house; thou

---

[1] *Od.*, vi, 8.     [2] *Od.*, vi, 204.     [3] *Od.*, vi, 4–6.

shalt see thy children, and may my name stand
well in thy city. . ." Then he heaps different
kinds of gifts upon his guest, who goes down to the
shore and embarks, after having rendered thanks
to his sovereign. Odysseus, also, receives good
wishes and presents from Alcinous and the Phæacians, to whom in return he renders thanks and
salutations.[1] Further, when the Shipwrecked
Mariner lands in his own country, "the bow of his
ship is run upon the shore"; and so with the Phæa-
eian crew, whose ship is grounded in such a fashion
that half of her keel rests on land.[2] Brought
unto Pharaoh, the Egyptian presents himself as a
man "who has seen much and suffered many
hardships"—words which are echoed in the burden
of Odysseus: "I have endured pain of heart in
passing through the wars of men and the grievous
waves of the sea." Even the epithet which the
Egyptian applies to himself, "the cautious servant" (aqer), is it not the prototype of the famous
πολύτροπος πολυμήχανος 'Οδυσσεὺς?

From the convincing parallelism, followed up
in detail by M. Golenischeff, I conclude, with him,
that "there must be more than a fortuitous
resemblance between the Egyptian tale and the
episode of Odysseus among the Phæacians." Nor

[1] Od., viii, 408; viii, 430; xiii, 10, 122, 135.    [2] Od., xiii, 113.

are the similarities confined to such particulars as might appear in any story of any shipwreck; but the two accounts reveal a common arrangement and plan. Nor is the incident of Odysseus to be compared with the Egyptian tale alone. M. Golenischeff has found all its essential features in one of the stories of *A Thousand and One Nights*, "The Seven Voyages of Sindbad the Sailor." Certain of the episodes in the Arab tale occur in the Homeric narrative, but are omitted from the Egyptian; contrariwise, others have been employed in the Odysseus recital, ascribing to the Cyclopes the adventures of the Phæacians; and, again, we find in the Arabian text certain features of the Egyptian story of which the Greek writer has not made use. These points of contact and of divergence between any two of the three stories led M. Golenischeff to suppose that the Homeric and Arab authors had not drawn directly upon their Egyptian ancestor, but that all three, Egyptian, Greek, Arab, had borrowed, each according to his own particular taste, from a common Oriental source, very ancient—since it must be prior to the Egyptian papyrus which dates from the XIIth dynasty, 2000 B.C. If we follow here the theories propounded by Helbig and Bérard, we conjecture this common source to be Asiatic, probably Phœnieian. Be this last hypothesis as it may, until some new and happy discovery puts us on the track of the archetype of the hieroglyphic, Greek, and Arabian texts, we must consider the Egyptian tale (at least provisionally) as the source of the Phæacian episode.

Not only did Homer borrow from Egyptian folk-lore, he seems also to have been inspired by Egyptian art. Helbig writes of the Shield of Achilles, that "the descriptions of certain scenes are inspired by plastic models. These models are chiefly metal vases of Phœnician importation or Greek imitations of such."[1] Limiting my inquiry to the first part of this proposition, I desire to investigate certain sources of Homeric inspiration and to discover whether these "plastic models" were not the funeral scenes of which thousands of examples are found in the forms of pictures or bas-reliefs in the Egyptian tombs, from the Memphite mastabas down to the Theban hypogea.[2]

[1] Helbig, *Das Homerische Epos*, 1890, p. 533.

[2] Murray (*History of Greek Sculpture*, 2d edition, 1890, p. 42 *et seq.*) has attempted a plastic reconstruction of the Shield, but the scenes he represents—harvest, dance, the hounds—are derived from Assyrian, Phœnician, Greek, and Egyptian models. He employs these different models in one and the same scene. Thus, in the attack of the flock by the lion, the flock is Assyrian; the lion, Phœnician; the dogs, Egyptian. Our comparisons rest exclusively on Egyptian pictures, generally complete in themselves.

To prove my argument, it is necessary to enter, again, the field of barren facts. I take, for my purpose, the scenes of rural life engraved upon the Shield of Achilles. "The representation," as pointed out by Brunn and Helbig, "is subdivided into as many pictures as there are seasons; the first depicts the tilling of the fields; the second, harvest; the third, vintage; the last, the shepherd's life."[1] On the Shield these pictures are supposed to succeed one another, or to be placed one above the other; likewise in the Egyptian tombs the scenes of ploughing, harvest, vintage, are placed in sequence on one wall of a hypogeum, or upon neighbouring walls, while the position of the pictures of shepherd life vary, being less characteristic of particular seasons than are the others.

It may be objected that although the subjects are the same, the poetical descriptions in the *Iliad* and the painted scenes on the funeral monuments are expressive of entirely different intentions. The Shield of Achilles is but a pretext for poetical descriptions, while the Egyptian pictures serve a definite religious purpose. If the artist portrays, on the walls of the tombs, scenes of tillage, harvest, vintage, it is not for decorative effect, but in order to bring before the eyes of the dead, who inhabit

[1] *Das Homerische Epos* (Leach, revised edition, p. 508).

the tomb, all the stages of the preparation of the
funeral offerings. The various and successive
phases of agricultural labour go on continually in
the next world, as they are fixed for ever on the
walls of the tomb, so that the dead may rest
assured that he will never lack for food. But
at the same time, in spite of the religious and
practical character of the work, the Egyptian
decorators treated their subjects from an artistic
standpoint and observed the rules of pictorial
composition. The subdivision into seasons with
the separate treatment of each was therefore as
necessary to the Egyptian decorator as to the
Greek poet; moreover, this method is referred to in
an inscription in a tomb at El Kab.[1]   Above the
scenes that we shall compare with the. Homeric
account, we read that "Paheri [the owner of the
tomb] gazes on the season of *Shemou* and the season
of *Pirit* and on all the works that are done in the
fields."[2]

[1] J. Tylor, *The Tomb of Paheri at El Kab*, Plate III (*Egypt.
Exploration Fund*, t. xi); *cf.* Brugsch, *Matériaux pour servir à la
reconstitution du calendrier*, p. 16.

[2] The Egyptian year was divided into three seasons of four
months; the inundation *Shâït* (from the end of July to the end of
November); the winter *Pirit* (from December to March); the
summer *Shemou* (from April to July). The field work took place
in winter (seedtime) and in summer (harvest). *Cf.* Brugsch, *Die
Aegyptologie*, pp. 357–361.

If the general arrangement of the Homeric descriptions corresponds to that of the Egyptian pictures, the analogy in the details of each scene is still more striking.

### Ploughing [1]

Furthermore he set in the shield a soft fresh-ploughed field, rich tilth and wide, the third time ploughed; *and many ploughers therein drave their yokes to and fro as they wheeled about.* Whensoever they came to the boundary of the field and turned, *then would a man come to each and give into his hands a goblet* of sweet wine, while others would be turning back along the furrows, fain to reach the boundary of the deep tilth. [2]

A ploughing scene of the same character has been represented in the Egyptian tombs from remotest times. The two essential and antithetic features of the Homeric version can be found in a picture in the hypogeum of Nakhti, [3] a priest attached to the service of Amon under the XVIIIth dynasty, about 1500 B.C. (Fig. 10). Observe:

1. The going to and fro of the ox-teams which cross the field from the outer boundary to a tree indicating the central point where each man wheels his plough about.

[1] *Iliad*, xviii, 541–547.      [2] Trans.: Lang, Leaf, and Myers.
[3] *Mémoires de la Mission archéologique française au Caire*, v. 3, p. 476 and Plate II.

2. The incident of the man who drinks. In the tomb of Nakhti, he drinks from a goat's skin which hangs from the boughs of a tree,[1] instead of from the Homeric goblet.

In the mastabas of the Vth and VIth dynasties,

FIG. 10.—Ploughing and Harvest (XVIIIth Dynasty).

the man who drinks appears, not in the ploughing, but in the harvest scene, where, on reaching the boundary of the field, he puts his sickle under his arm and carries an elongated vessel to his lips (Fig. 13).[2] Slight variations of the Homeric ploughman are found in the Egyptian pictures of

[1] From a tomb at El Kab (Erman, *Aegypten*, p. 575), and Wilkinson, *Manners and Customs*, ii, p. 419.

[2] Wilkinson, *Manners and Customs*, ii, p. 419.

the harvest. In the tombs at Zaouït-el-Meïtin,[1] of the Vth and VIth dynasties, about 2600 B.C., a man comes to meet a harvester at the boundary of the field and with both hands holds out to him a vessel that his companion may drink (Fig. 12). The motive was familiar enough to the Egyptian decorators, and it seems likely that some day from

FIG. 11.—A Goat's-Skin.

FIG. 12.—Sharing the Drinking-Cup (VIth Dynasty).

among the hundreds of similar scenes that have been found in mastabas and hypogea and are yet unpublished, there will turn up ploughing-scenes which correspond to the one described in Homer.

## Harvest [2]

Furthermore he set therein a *demesne-land deep in corn, where hinds were reaping with sharp sickles in their hands. Some armfuls along the swathe were falling in rows to the earth, while others the sheaf-binders were binding in twisted bands of straw.* Three sheaf-binders

[1] Lepsius, *Denkmäler*, ii, 106 b.    [2] *Iliad*, xviii, 550–560.

stood over them, *while behind, boys gathering corn,*
*bearing it in their arms gave it constantly to the binders;*
*and among them the lord in silence was standing at the*

FIG. 13.—Harvesters (XVIIIth Dynasty).

*swathe with his staff, rejoicing in his heart.*    And hench-
men apart beneath an oak *were making ready a feast,*
and *preparing a great ox they had sacrificed;* while the
women were strewing much white barley to be a
supper for the hinds.[1]

All the essential features of this description
occur in the Egyptian pictures of the harvest.

FIG. 14.—Reapers and Gleaners (XVIIth Dynasty).

Again, in the hypogeum of Nakhti (Fig. 10), we
see above the ploughman, three reapers cutting
with their sickles the ears of corn, which stand as
high as their heads; behind them, a little girl stoops
to gather the ears of corn which she puts in a little

[1] Trans.: Lang, Leaf, and Myers.

basket; above, the binders bind closely together
by means of a cord and a stick the sheaves which
lie heaped in a great wicker basket, while, on their
left, two girls are plucking flax (Fig. 10). In
contrast with the Homeric description, here, the
children glean for themselves, instead of binding
up the sheaves for the reapers; the same thing

FIG. 15.—Binders (Vth Dynasty).     FIG. 16.—The Master.

occurs in a picture in the Paheri's tomb[1] (Fig.
14), where two little girls are seen gleaning, the
first saying to the men who are reaping the corn:
"Give me a handful. . . ." (Egyptian: DOT,
*manipulus* sheaf). But in other pictures, the
reapers are helped by other workmen who hold up
the sheaves for those who bind them together;[2]
sometimes it is the flax stalks which are being
made all the same length before they are bound
together. Finally, in a Memphite mastaba, we see

[1] J. Tylor, *The Tomb of Paheri*, Plate III.
[2] Lepsius, *Denkmäler*, ii, 106 *b*.

the corn cut by the sickle, falling in rows along the swathe,[1] as in Homer (Fig. 17). We should further notice, inserted in several harvest scenes, the motives of the man who quenches his thirst, two variants of which occur in Figures 12 and 14, upon which comments have already been made.[2]

As for the meal prepared by the Homeric κήρυκες, it has its exact equivalent in the dismemberment

FIG. 17.—Reapers (Vth Dynasty).

of the sacrificial bull by the sacrificial slaughterers, portrayed in a corner of the picture in the tomb of Nakhti. In Egypt, as in Homeric Greece, every meal is also a sacrifice, and the epithet given to the men who prepare the Homeric repast, ἱερεύσαντες, can also be applied to the Egyptian slaughterers. Here, in the tomb, it is, primarily a meal for the deceased that is in course

---

[1] Dümichen, *Resultate der archaelog. photograph. Expedition,* Plate X. See also Newberry, *Beni-Hasan,* i, Plate 29.

[2] In Nakhti's tomb, we see above the picture of the harvest, one of the measuring of the corn in bushels and the threshing of it—the last stages of the preparation of the cereal offerings.

of preparation (Fig. 10), and the dismemberment is a preparatory stage before the offering of the thighs, which are seen above upon the sacrificial pile. The essential point to notice is that the sacrifice of the bull, portrayed here, above the harvest scene and on the boundary of the field, is presented, as in the *Iliad*, as a necessary aecompaniment of the labour of the field. Finally, let it be observed, how Nakhti and his wife pour a libation from a wide-throated bottle upon the pile of varied offerings, and which owing to the faulty perspective of the drawing, appears to flow down, at the same time, upon the slaughtered bull. Does not their action recall the women of Homer? Does it not appear as if they were "strewing the supper" with liquid flour?

No less characteristic in both picture and poetic description is the presence of the master, standing erect, silent, his staff in his hand. Speaking correctly, Nakhti is not standing, but is seated beneath a light summer tent, such as Egyptians used to pitch in their fields (Fig 10); but, elsewhere, the dead, while contemplating the labour, for the production of his funeral offering, is represented in a standing attitude (Fig. 16). Even the Greek idiotism, γηθόσυνος χῆρ, "rejoicing in his heart," has its literal counterpart in the hieroglyphic commentary upon scenes of this character. Continually, above such pictures, words like these are found: "He (the lord of the tomb) sees, and *rejoices in his heart (skhem àb)* to see the labours of the field."[1]

### Vintage[2]

Also he set therein a vineyard teeming plenteously with clusters, wrought in fair gold; *black were the grapes, but the vines hung throughout on silver poles.* And *around it he ran a ditch of cyanus* and *round that a fence of tin;* and *one single pathway led to it, whereby the vintagers might go when they should gathér the vintage.* And *maidens and striplings* in childish glee *bare the sweet fruit in plaited baskets.*[3]

In the tomb of Nakhti, the picture of the vintage faces those of ploughing and harvest (Fig. 18). Here, as in the vintage scenes[4] of the VIth and

----

[1] Above the representation of Nakhti seated in his summer-house is inscribed, "Act of sitting in the summer-house and of viewing the demesne lands on behalf of. . . ." The expression *skhem àb* occurs in the vintage picture.

[2] *Iliad.*, xviii, 561–568.     [3] Trans.: Lang, Leaf, and Myers.

[4] Above the vine-arbour in the tomb of Phtahhetep (Dümichen, *Resultate* . . . Plate VIII) we read the phrase *ouha àaririt* "to gather the grape, to reap the vintage"; the word "grape" *àaririt* is "determined" by the vine,.represented by a stock, the shoots of which are propped up by two poles. Under the New Empire, a Theban tomb, called "the tomb of the vines," affords characteristic illustrations of the Egyptian vine. Here the walls and ceiling of each chamber are ornamented with the vine-arbour (published by M. Virey in the *Recueil de travaux relatifs à la philologie égyptienne* (t. xx–xxii).

VIIth dynasties, the vineyard is an arched arbour, in which the vines are supported by vertical and horizontal cross-poles from which fall the heavily laden branches (Fig. 19). On the Shield, also, the vine forms a long arched arbour, supported throughout its length by poles, with a single alleyway running through it. The vintagers of Nakhti, likewise, have room only for two to walk abreast. In the tomb of Phtahhetep, one man gathers the grapes from low down on the left, another from low down on the right; both stoop, from lack of space to stand upright, while a child,

FIG. 18.—The Vintage (between Hunting and Fishing) (XVIIIth Dynasty).

gathering from the side of the arbour, stands and plucks the grapes with both his hands. We see the bunches placed in plaited baskets and borne to the wine-press. Thus, the Homeric

16

FIG. 19.—The Vintage and Sports.

vine, in its essential features, recalls the Egyptian (Fig. 19).

The Greek text adds a Bacchic chorus, which is missing from the Egyptian pictures: "And in their midst a boy made pleasant music on a clear-toned viol, and sang thereto a sweet Linos-song[1] with delicate voice; while the rest, with feet falling together, kept time with the music and song." The Egyptian tombs show us no singing boy beside the vineyard, no viol, no dancing chorus, but there is the wine-press in which vintagers holding on with one hand to a beam or to a cord (Fig. 18 and 19) tread the grapes rhythmically.[2] It is probable that they used also songs and shouts to give a measure to their movements. One of the bas-reliefs in the tomb of Phtahhetep shows us children playing, wrestling, turning somersaults, while the hieroglyphic legend (*gah* (?) *àaririt*) sets forth

---

[1] Probably a lament for departing summer.
[2] The Egyptian tombs very often show by the side of pictures of the preparation of offerings, scenes of pleasure, dance, and instrumental music. Even where the decorator is cramped for space, he wedges in the dance scene. In the Louvre, three stelæ, C 16, 17, 18, reproduce in miniature the decorations of the tomb of a certain Ousirtasen who lived under the XIIth dynasty. On stele C 18, the deceased is engaged in hunting and surveying the labours of the field; on stele C 17, he receives one by one the funeral offerings, while a maiden dances to the accompaniment of harps and hand-clapping. Murray has reproduced one of these Egyptian dances in his reconstruction of the Shield.

that these rejoicings are connected with the vintage time.

Finally, there are some curious analogies in the setting of these scenes. The Homeric vine is surrounded by "a ditch of cyanus" (κυανέην κάπετον), and around that "a fence of tin" (ἕρκος κασσιτέρου). Now, the vineyard in the tomb of Nakhti is surrounded, above and below, by scenes of fishing and marsh - hunting, so that the walls appear bounded by deep ditches in which grow thick rushes. This characteristic marsh landscape is a traditional setting for vintage scenes. Wine was associated, for the Egyptians, with a particular kind of scenery. They drank their wine in summer-houses on the edge of the waters, where they snared birds or fished with nets or harpoons. Therefore, the scenes relating to the funeral offering of wine are those of marsh fishing, or of the decoy of marsh birds. If the dead has ever before his eyes pools, water-thickets, and vineyards, it is because these pleasant places were always found near to one another in his earthly life, as they are on the walls of his tomb. It is of interest, therefore, that the Homeric vine should be likewise encircled by a bluish ditch and a fence of whitish hue, as if it might have been set in water and a thicket of reeds.

## The Attack of the Oxen by Lions[1]

Also he wrought therein a herd of kine with upright horns, and the kine were fashioned of gold and tin, and with lowing they hurried from the byre to pasture beside a murmuring river, beside the waving reed. And herdsmen of gold were following with the kine, four of them, and nine dogs fleet of foot came after them. But two terrible lions among the foremost kine had seized a loud-roaring bull that bellowed mightily as they hailed him, and the dogs and the young men sped after him. The lions rending the great bull's hide were devouring his vitals and his black blood while the herdsmen in vain tarred on their fleet dogs to set on, for they shrank from biting the lions but stood hard by and barked and swerved away.[2]

The characteristic features of this description are produced in only a few pictures of the Egyptian tombs. Pastoral scenes occur constantly in the Memphite mastabas and the hypogea of Beni-Hasan and El-Bersheh;[3] but the essential point of comparison, the attack of the lion, is missing. On the contrary, a picture in the mastaba of Phtahhetep[4] gives us, beneath the vintage, a hunting-scene in which occurs the Homeric motive of the lion. The incident takes place in an undulating part of the desert, and not on the banks

---

[1] *Iliad*, xviii, 573–586.          [2] Trans.: Lang, Leaf, and Myers.
[3] Newberry, *Beni-Hasan*, ii, Plate 12.
[4] Dümichen, *Resultate* . . „ Plate VIII.

of a river. Moreover, it would appear to be a
lion-hunt with a live bull serving as a bait, rather
than the attack upon a flock by a lion.    Yet the
group of the lion and the bellowing bull whose
bowels are moved with terror, and the group of the
hunter or ox-herd exciting the fleet greyhounds
which "swerve away," prudently sheltering them-

FIG. 20.—The Attack of the Bull by the Lion (Vth Dynasty).

selves behind their master, invite comparison
(Fig. 20).

The motive of a lion seizing upon a bull was
treated in other works of art.    On an Egyptian
axe in the Berlin Museum, we see the lion seizing
the bull by the muzzle as in the funeral picture.[1]
On a bronze cup in the Cairo Museum, we see a
flock grazing on the banks of the Nile, where the
fish leap high and the reeds grow tall; the cattle
are chewing the cud, a cow suckles her calf, when,
suddenly, a lion dashes into their midst, and hurls
himself at the head of one of the animals.[2]

[1] G. Steindorff, *Die Blütezeit des Pharaonenreiches* (1900), p. 56.
[2] *Jahrbuch des kaiserl. deutsch. archaeol. Instituts*, Bd. xiii,
1898, I.   *Cf.* Steindorff, p. 134.

To sum up, the scenes on the Shield dealing with agricultural life recall, in their general arrangement as well as in certain particular details, a number of Egyptian pictures scattered among the tombs of all periods, or collected in one monument, as in the hypogeum of Nakhti. Brunn and Helbig have already pointed out that each of these scenes was "enhanced by antithetic arrangement."[1] The ploughmen work energetically, but each one, at the end of the furrow, is refreshed with a cup of wine; the reapers cut the corn and bind it into sheaves— opposite them the master stands idle, overseeing the labour of his servants; the vintagers pluck the ripe grapes—beside them others make song and music. The same well-balanced contrasts are exhibited on the walls of the mastabas and hypogeas; in the pictures of the harvest, in particular, the antitheses are carefully carried out. Elsewhere we find the Homeric motives differently treated; many details of the Egyptian pictures have been misunderstood or omitted from the Homeric description, while it is sometimes the Greek text that carries on the development. Such differences can be easily explained. The Egyptian sculptor or painter had to fit his designs to the space they would occupy upon the wall; often he had to sub-

[1] *L'épopée homérique,* p. 508.

ordinate his choice of details to their religious significance, while the poet need bring into his poetical descriptions only essential or artistic elements.  On the other hand, the painter and sculptor are limited to the presentment of a particular action at a particular moment, while the poet can present his subject in its entirety, from the beginning of the action to its end.  Therefore, the difference of treatment by painter and poet cannot be advanced as an argument against the hypothesis that the Homeric treatment was based upon an Egyptian model.  As Helbig has correctly surmised, "plastic reminiscence, poetic expression,—these are two elements which must be considered in explaining the details of these descriptions."[1]

It only remains to be asked how the imagination of the Homeric Bards came under the influence of Egyptian art.  Was it through the channel of Phœnician works of art?  Knowing the influence Egypt exercised over Phœnician art, this view is worthy of consideration.  But was it not possible that the Greeks should have had personal knowledge of the Egyptian models?  We know that the ancient necropolis, at Memphis and elsewhere,

[1] L'épopée homérique, p. 329.

attracted visitors,[1] and the Greeks, whom we know had free access into Egypt, would not be the less eager to penetrate the mysteries of the tombs. Be that as it may, the Homeric Bards seem to have been familiar with Egyptian funeral bas-reliefs or pictures, or imitations of them. But through what channel the influence came is not, at this moment, our concern. We wish only to point out that there was such influence. We do not presume to say that we have discovered, among the innumerable funeral pictures, the actual originals that inspired the Greek poet. But we ask to be permitted to draw the conclusion that upon the Shield of Achilles are presented, with a remarkable fidelity, decorative motives that were employed in Egypt from the time of the first dynasties.

[1] From the VIth dynasty (see Mariette, *Les Mastabas*, p. 417), there appears on the funeral stelæ a formula of, probably, still earlier date, concerning "the living who come to the tomb." These are of every condition, and not relatives, but visitors who come to the necropolis simply out of curiosity. The *Tale of Satni-Kahmoïs*, written in Ptolemaic times, depicts personages of the XIXth dynasty sightseeing among the tombs and making comments upon the pictures and inscriptions. We often find in the tombs Egyptian or Greek *graffiti*—testimonies of these visits.

# CHAPTER VIII

## THE READING OF HIEROGLYPHICS

"HER beauty remains hidden; none could lift her veil." This line from a hymn to Isis might, until the end of the nineteenth century, have been applied to Egypt. Here was a land offering to the visitor astounding monuments which appealed to the artistic taste of even the uncultivated, but man's intelligence was baffled by the bewildering tracery of birds, animals, and lines wrought into the stones. Since the Emperor Theodosius, at the end of the fourth century, had closed the temples for worship and dispersed the priesthood of Osiris and Amon, the secret of this pictorial script had been lost. The Christian Copts, indeed, had continued to speak the dialects of ancient Egypt, but as they used the Greek alphabet when writing them, those pictorial signs which the Greeks called *hieroglyphics*, fell into oblivion.

Seven centuries of Greek and Roman rule in Egypt had sufficed to bring about, progressively, the decay of the language and the national civilisation, and the abandonment of the old script. Though the Greeks felt a keen interest in the Egyptian religion and philosophy, they appear to have been disheartened by the difficulties of the language. Herodotus, Diodorus, Strabo, who visited Egypt and have left descriptions of her customs and institutions, were content with second-hand information—not always reliable—from the lips of interpreters. Their knowledge of the writing seems to have been very superficial. Herodotus says:[1] "There are two kinds of characters; one is called sacred, the other popular." Diodorus[2] confirms this statement: "The priests teach the youth two sorts of letters; the 'sacred,' used by the priests, and others which are for the common purposes of life." Modern science has borrowed from this tradition—a tradition only half-true—two expressions for the two forms of Egyptian characters; the *hieroglyphic* writing, engraved on monuments, and the *demotic* writing used for everyday purposes.

There were, however, certain Greeks who approached the problem of the Egyptian language.

[1] Herodotus, ii, 36.      [2] Diodorus, i, 6.   Trans.: G. Booth.

Diogenes Laertius says that Democritus, one of the Ionian philosophers, about 450 B.C., had written dissertations upon the hieroglyphics of Meroe and the texts engraved on an obelisk of Memphis. We also possess a few extracts of a hieroglyphic dictionary compiled by Cheremon, a keeper of the Library of the Serapeum in the first century A.D.[1] We learn, for example, that the idea of joy was expressed by the figure of a woman playing on a dulcimer, that a bow stood for swiftness, and the idea of old age was rendered by the outline of an old man. It was on the ground of this limited knowledge, true as far as it went in this case, that it was for a long time believed that hieroglyphics were signs standing for objects or ideas; that is to say, were ideographs or symbolic characters. Another treatise on *Hieroglyphics* composed in Egyptian by a native called Horus, and translated into Greek about 250 B.C., by Philippus, under the title of *Hieroglyphica of Horapollon*,[2] gives us in two books the symbolic explanation of 189 hieroglyphics. Many of these interpretations are true; for example, a stem represents the year; a goose,

---

[1] Fragments of Cheremon were found by Birch in a compilation made by the Byzantine monk Tzetzes, about 1000 A.D.

[2] See the edition of the *Hieroglyphica* by Leemans, Leyden, 1836.

the word son; a hawk stands for mother; an ostrich feather symbolises justice.   But it is self-evident that the small number of signs explained by Horapollon would be of little service to the moderns in their attempts at deciphering.

Hieroglyphics did not consist of symbols only. Clement of Alexandria, one of the most learned scholars among the Church Fathers, leaves a valuable testimony to this at the end of the first century, at a time when many Egyptians still made use of hieroglyphics.

At the outset Clement formulates with precision the fact that there are various writings, in the following terms: "The Egyptian pupils are first taught *epistolography*, the writing reserved for ordinary intercourse (now termed *demotic*); next they are taught the *hieratic* style which is employed by the sacred scribes or hierographers; lastly *hieroglyphics*." Unfortunately, the author omits to state, what would have been of considerable import to the decipherers, whether these three modes of writing, which we call to-day *demotic, hieratic, hieroglyphic*, made use of three different types of characters or were modifications of one common one. This omission made Egyptian script, according to Clement, appear still more complex than according to Herodotus or Diodorus, since he introduced a third form of character, the *hieratic*, by the side of the demotic and the hieroglyphic.

But Clement adds puzzle to puzzle by the explanation he gives of the hieroglyphic script, properly so called. "There are two kinds of hieroglyphics; the one is *cyriologic* (by that is meant signs used with their proper, non-figurative meaning) and employs the first alphabetical letters; the other is *symbolic.*"

Clement says nothing more about the cyriological hieroglyphs. We must wait for Champollion to explain to us the riddle of "the first alphabetical letters." But he enters into details concerning the symbolic hieroglyphics.

The symbolic hieroglyphs are written in many ways. The first expresses objects by their graphic representation. Thus: when the Egyptians wish to write the sun, they draw a circle; to write the moon they draw a crescent.

The second method expresses the object in a tropical (figurative) form. This tropical method changes or deviates the meaning of objects by the employment of analogy, and expresses them by modifying or transforming their image in various ways. Thus they make use of *anaglyphs* when they want to sing the praises of their kings under the guise of religious myths.

The third method consists entirely of allegories expressed by certain enigmas.  Here is an example of such an enigmatic allusion: The Egyptians represent all the *other* stars by serpents, on account of their oblique course, but the sun is represented by a scarab.[1]

Clement's testimony brings forward a point of cardinal importance.  He makes us understand—though in obscure terms—that the hieroglyphic signs are not exclusively, as Cheremon and Horapollon seemed to believe, ideographs and symbols.  A sign may be a letter; it may stand for an object; or it may convey a symbolic meaning by direct or indirect allusion.  The problem is thus stated in all its complexity.  But if this passage of the *Stromateis*—which was not understood— set forth the difficulties of the problem, it gave no clue to its solution.  These difficulties may be summed up in three questions:

1.  Is the Egyptian language, in its threefold script, one or complex?

2.  How are we to distinguish the three values, —alphabetical, ideographical, and symbolical,— represented by the signs?

3.  When the value of the signs has been ascertained, with what sounds are they read; how

[1] *Stromateis* (ap. Champollion, *Précis du système hiéroglyphique* (1824), p. 328)

can we separate the sentences, isolate the words, and distinguish grammatical forms and functions?

Towards the end of the Renaissance, a few curious minds, following the lead of the archæologists and philologists who had laboured upon the monuments of classical antiquity, applied themselves to the examination of the Sphinx of Egypt. The Jesuit Father, Kircher, at the beginning of the seventeenth century, attempted to revive the study of the Coptic language. It was something more than luck; rather was it genius which revealed to him that, hidden under its guise of a Greek spelling and writing, Coptic continued the old Egyptian language. He discovered that Coptic is not only related to the ancient mother tongue of Egypt, but springs from it, is, indeed, but a later form of it, transcribed into Greek writing. But it was not possible to go back from Coptic to the old mother tongue, as we can, for instance, from French to Latin, until the phonetic reading of the hieroglyphic was known. And the key to this mysterious writing was lost. Working on the suggestions of Horapollon, Kircher sought for, or divined, ideas, but not sounds, in the hieroglyphics. Trusting to his own perspicuity, he read into the signs what he wanted them to say.

For instance, on the Pamphilian obelisk the Emperor Domitian is given simply the Greek title of *Autocrator* expressed in hieroglyphics, but Kircher translated it:"Osiris is the agent of fruitfulness and of vegetation, and this creative power was a gift from Heaven conferred upon him during his reign by the holy Mophta."

Such a guess-work system proved more harmful to Egyptology than serviceable, and it was not until the end of the eighteenth century that critical methods were employed by De Guignes and Zoega. De Guignes, comparing the Egyptian hieroglyphic with the Chinese characters, traced in the Egyptian the existence of *determinative* characters, that is, of ideograms without phonetic value, used at the end of words to "determine" and define their general meaning. The Dane, Zoega, opposing Kircher's system, showed that hieroglyphics more often stood for sounds and that they should be regarded as mere letters, instead of each sign being made the symbol of a mysterious language, the vehicle of transcendental ideas.

About the same time, interest was aroused in Europe by the Egyptian monuments brought thither. The French and German art critics— Caylus and Winckelmann—discuss the Egyptian

obelisks and statuary in their Collections of Antiquities. The store of hieroglyphic inscriptions
began to increase, owing to the travels in the East
of men like Paul Lucas (1603), Norden (1741),
Pocoke (1743), and Niebuhr (1788), who made
collections on the spot; but as yet the texts were
not properly understood and the copies of them
were so faulty that to-day they are almost useless;
but they reveal how Egypt exercised a fascination
upon the minds of men, and how they were attracted to her by the mystery of her inscriptions and
the beauty of her monuments. In 1798, when
Bonaparte entered upon his military campaign in
Egypt, he took with him a scientific commission,
including scholars, artists, and surveyors, to
whom was entrusted the charge of drawing, surveying, and studying tombs and temples. When
Egypt was conquered, Bonaparte established in
Cairo, side by side with the civil and military
authorities, an Egyptian Academy—*L'Institut d'*
*Égypte*—to maintain the principle that in this
illustrious land, science, no less than politics, had a
vast and invaluable conquest to achieve. During
the three years of the French occupation, scholars
like Jomard and De Villiers drew up, amid great
difficulties but with indomitable enthusiasm and
perseverance, an inventory of the archæological

treasures of Egypt. In 1808, after the scholars of the Egyptian Institute had been driven out of the Nile Valley, they began to publish the results of their labours in that magnificent *Description of Egypt*, which provides a land-survey of its ancient and modern monuments, and which, even to-day, affords an inexhaustible mine of information.

In the month of August, 1799, a man in Bonaparte's army, Bouchard, a Captain of the Engineers, found near Rosetta, a basalt stele, on which three inscriptions were engraved: one in pictorial signs, another in lineal signs, the third in Greek characters. The Greek text stated that here were three versions—in hieroglyphic, demotic, and Greek—of a decree of the Egyptian priests in honour of Ptolemy Epiphany and his wife Cleopatra in 196 B.C. The top of the tablet, bearing a part of the hieroglyphic text, had been broken away, but still there was an Egyptian inscription in two writings; the meaning was clear by the key that the Greek afforded; it remained to analyse and decipher the unknown scripts.

It was the demotic to which scholars first turned their attention, probably because its cursive characters, with their resemblance to Arabic, are more in accord with our habitual conception of writing than the pictorial signs. As early as 1802 the great French Orientalist, Silvestre de Sacy,[1] demonstrated that demotic was a practical and popular form of writing which contained no "riddles" and in which the signs, purely alphabetical and not ideographic, stood for letters, that is, for sounds— a theory that was only half-true. He classified all the forms of signs and reduced them to an alphabet of twenty-five demotic letters; next he endeavoured to distinguish in his text groups of similar signs forming words that occurred repeatedly in the text. Guided by the Greek, Sacy succeeded in finding out approximately in the demotic the place of the royal names, and in reading *Ptolemy, Berenice, Alexander, Arsinoe.* But such a method was too mechanical not to bring errors in its train. Thus Sacy interpreted the circle within which the royal names are inscribed as a letter. The Swedish scholar Ackerblad[1] in pointing out this mistake fell into another, when he interpreted this graphic ornament as a definite article.

A period of seventeen years followed these researches before an Englishman, Dr. Thomas Young, attacked the hieroglyphic portion of the

---

[1] *Lettre au citoyen Chaptal,* 1802.
[1] *Lettre sur l' inscription égyptienne du monument de Rosette,* 1802.

inscription. Pursuing the methods of Sacy and Ackerblad, who had first identifiéd names of persons in the demotic text, being guided thereto by the positions of their Greek equivalents, Dr. Young identified portions of the two royal names: *Ptolmis*-Ptolemy and *Birniks*-Berenice, in attributing to the signs the following values:[1]

Pt . . . . ole ma e osh   Bir e n e . . . . ke . . . .

It must be remarked that in the two names many signs were not identified. Young dismissed these as superfluous or inexplicable, which amounts to a confession of the failure of the mechanical method. Young was not successful with other royal names. Where there stood *Evergetes* and *Autocrator*, he read Cæsar and Arsinoe. As another English scholar put it, "Young proceeded by induction and clung with blind obstinacy to a faulty hypothesis."

At last appeared a Frenchman of genius, Jean François Champollion (born in 1791), who borrowing from his predecessors, Zoega, De Sacy, Ackerblad, and Young, "his first exact notions," discovered almost at one stroke the correct solution of all the different elements of the problem. As a schoolboy he had devoted himself with passion to the study of Coptic, and now, recog-

---

[1] See *Account of Discoveries in Hieroglyphical Literature*, 1823.

nising the profundity of Kircher's inspiration that
Coptic was the Egyptian language in disguise,
he sought to find, behind the mask of the Greek
alphabet, the phonetic reading of the Egyptian
words.

However, until 1821, Champollion held hieroglyphic writing to be symbolic, and not alphabetic.
But between the years 1821 and 1822 he changed
his opinion, perhaps under the influence of the
results obtained by Young in the reading of royal
names.   The new discovery of a bilingual inscription was also a determining factor. ˙ In January,
1822, the French scholars learned of a hieroglyphic
text inscribed on the base of a little obelisk in
Philæ, which had already supplied a Greek inscription.   Champollion first concentrated his examination upon the hieroglyphics that were surrounded
by a cartouche ⊂⊐, for Zoega had  demonstrated
that the cartouche appertains only to royal names.
These names, according to the Greek text, were
Cleopatra and Ptolemy.   The names had three
signs in common, and Champollion inferred that
these common signs ought to stand for the letters
*p t l* which occur in both cartouches.   This
established Young's theory that the characters
with which royal names are written correspond to
alphabetical letters and have no symbolic value.

This theory that Young discovered by chance received scientific demonstration from Champollion. There flashed upon his mind that obscure statement of Clement of Alexandria: "A kind of hieroglyphic, called cyriologic, employs the first alphabetical letters; the other kind is symbolic." Another scholar, Letronne, helped him to interpret these words. Since Young and Champollion had proved the royal names to be written in signs that were not symbolical, it followed that they were *cyriological*. The next step for Champollion to discover was for what "first letters" the hieroglyphs composing the names *Cleopatra* and *Ptolemy* should stand. He judged it was necessary to establish what was the object imitated or represented by each sign. He identified this object, then looked for its name in Coptic. Then he discovered that every phonetic hieroglyph stood for the sound of the *first letter* of the Egyptian or Coptic word.[1]

[1] *Cf.* Champollion, *Précis du système hiéroglyphique* (1824): "Any phonetic hierogylph is the picture of an object the name of which, in the spoken Egyptian, began with the utterance, the articulation of the very sound that the sign itself was meant to represent." Letronne, who, on behalf of Champollion, commented upon Clement of Alexandria, translated the *"cyriologic"* signs thus: "characters used for expressing objects in *their proper meaning* by means of the first alphabetic letters."

But what kind of first letters? Letronne suggested, from a text of Plutarch, that Clement meant hieroglyphic signs corre-

I give below an example to illustrate Champollion's method of decipherment, as Birch has already done:

1. The first sign in the cartouche of Cleopatra is the figure of a knee, in Coptic, "*kelle*" or "*keli*"; *K* should therefore be the initial of the name and it does not occur in Ptolemy.

2. The second sign, a crouching lion, in Egyptian, "*labou*," in Coptic, "*laboi*," is an *L*. It is

---

sponding to the sounds of the first sixteen letters of the Greek alphabet. Though Champollion refers to the authority of Letronne, his own understanding of Clement's text is different; for him the words διὰ τῶν πρώτων στοιχείων designate merely the *initial* letters of certain Egyptian words which served to form the Egyptian phonetic alphabet (cf. *Grammaire*, p. 28). This interpretation was supported by Goulianoff (*Essai sur les hiéroglyphes*, 1827); but the Russian thought erroneously that by this system he would be able to read most of the hieroglyphs. Klaproth translated with exactness the passage of the *Stromateis* by: "cyriologic by means of *initial letters*" and built up a theory of "acrologic" signs in which by the side of the correct views he placed certain errors, exposed by Champollion ("Première et deuxième lettre sur la découverte des hiéroglyphes acrologiques," 1827, *Bulletin universel des sciences*, April, 1827).

found, with this value, in the fourth place in the name Ptolemy (Young read the lion as *ole*).

3.   The third sign, a reed in Coptic, "*ake*," stands for *E* (A) in Cleopatra and occurs in the sixth and seventh places in Ptolemy (Ptolmais) where it represents a diphthong: *AI* or *AIO*.

4.   The fourth sign, a kind of knot, stands for *O* in Cleopatra, and serves the same purpose in the third place in Ptolemy (Young considered this a "superfluous" sign).

5.   The fifth sign, a mat, which stands for *P* in Cleopatra, is the first letter in Ptolemy.

6.   The sixth sign, an eagle, in Coptic, "*ahom*," does not occur in Ptolemy, but it occurs again for *A* in the sixth and ninth place in Cleopatra.

7.   The seventh sign which represents a hand, in Coptic, "*toot*," stands, certainly, for *T* in Cleopatra, though it is not to be found in Ptolemy. Champollion had already recognised the existence of "homophones," that is, of different signs bearing the same reading.

8.   The eighth sign is a mouth, in Coptic "*ro*"; it fulfils the function of the consonant *R*.

9.   The ninth sign repeats the eagle *A*, already explained.

10–11.   Finally, the segment ▬ second sign in Ptolemy and the egg ◖, which often occur

together ⬤ ● at the end of feminine names seemed
not, in the opinion of Champollion, to serve any
phonetic purpose in the word Cleopatra.    The *t*,
an index of the feminine, corresponds to the *t*, feminine article in Coptic.    The egg is a determinative
sign of the feminine gender.

Thus all the signs, except the *M* and the *S*, had
been identified in their regular sequence, and it
was as legitimate, as easy, to assign the values
*M* and *S* to the two signs (⬅ and 𝟙) that
remain unidentified.

In his *Lettre à M. Dacier*, secretary to L'Académie des Inscriptions (1822), Champollion published the result of his methodical analysis, so
different from the hazardous and mechanical
method practised by Dr. Young.    On other points
also he broke away from his predecessors; he no
longer regarded demotic as a different script from
the hieratic and hieroglyphic, he regarded it rather
as a true "tachigraphy of the hieroglyphic."    The
conclusions already reached by Sacy and Young
were that in the demotic text signs expressed
sounds not ideas.    If it were true that demotic
was but a cursive derivation from the hieroglyphic,
the latter would include with ideograms, signs
standing for sounds; in a word, there would be
phonetic hieroglyphs.    Moreover, the monuments

of the Græco-Roman period bore the names of the Ptolemies and the Cæsars, of which we know the sound. If, now, in these names written in hieroglyphics, the same sounds were found always to be represented by the same letters, this phonetic alphabet would be proved correct, as already in the cartouches of Cleopatra and Ptolemy. By this method, Champollion read seventy-nine royal names, in which, in contrast to Young, he succeeded in interpreting every letter. With the aid of this list, Champollion was able, at one stroke, to draw up an almost definitive alphabet of phonetic hieroglyphs.

Thus far, Champollion had confined his study to royal names and particularly those of the Græco-Roman period. He and others were stubbornly prepossessed by the idea that the names of the Ptolemies and the Cæsars were written in alphabetic signs because the Egyptian scribes knew no other way to transcribe foreign names from a language which possessed no ideographs. But, it was urged, the real national Egyptian language would surely employ only symbolic characters, such as Clement of Alexandria opposes to the cyriologic signs. Champollion, however, abandoned that attitude.

A glance at the Rosetta stone shows that most of
the hieroglyphs that compose the greater part of the
Egyptian inscription are the same as also compose
the names of foreign rulers and they are grouped in
different ways.    For instance, the cartouche surrounding the name of *Pt*olemy contains the group
⸱⸱⟨⟩ ❧ ⟨⟨ in which the first two signs are the first two
hieroglyphs of the name of *Pt*olemy, that is *P* and *T*.
But the Greek version contains the epithet ἠγαπήμενος
ὐπὸ τοῦ Φθᾶ "beloved of Phtah" (Coptic, *Ptah*); hence
it follows that the third hieroglyph ❧ represents *H*.[1]

Acting on this principle, Champollion read a
certain number of words, of which he found the
meaning and phonetic equivalents in Coptic.    He
was thus able to compile, beside the alphabet, the
first dictionary of hieroglyphs and a grammar[2] of
the Egyptian language, deduced from Coptic.

Following the guidance of his genius, and pursuing this method of scientific analysis, Champollion advanced by giant strides along the unbeaten
track.    The vista, opened out to him, was far
wider than he had at first imagined it would be.
Contrary to his earlier theory, he discovered that
the phonetic hieroglyphs were not an invention for
the transcription of the names of foreign sovereigns, but had been in use, since the remotest

[1] The vowel *a* is not accounted for; the vowels not being written
in Egyptian.
[2] The *Grammar* was published in 1836; the *Dictionary* in 1841.

times. The name *Khoufou* (Greek, *Cheops*), the builder of the Great Pyramid, was written at the time of the IVth dynasty with the very same alphabetical signs. Thus, not only a portion of Egyptian antiquity, but the *whole* of Egyptian civilisation with its innumerable documents, was an open book in which he could read. He held the key which gave him access to its language at every stage of its development, at all periods of its existence. By the aid of the Coptic language, as codified in dictionaries and lexicons, he had been able to trace many words back to their roots, and so arrive at their original meaning. Thus he was able to divide the hieroglyphic text into separate words and to identify grammatical forms. Then the hieroglyphic language stood revealed in all its fulness, with the fourfold value of its hieroglyphs as letters, or alphabetical signs, as syllables, or syllabic signs, as summarised ideas, or ideographic signs, and lastly its signs added to the ends of words to define their exact meaning, or determinative signs.

Thus, within ten years, Champollion had surveyed the whole subject and had resolved its various problems. He had demonstrated how the threefold script, demotic, hieratic, hieroglyphic, sprang from one common stock of picture-writing.

From the chaos of pictorial signs, he had separated the alphabet, the symbols, the determinatives. His thorough knowledge of Coptic illuminated for him the obscure cyriologic process alluded to by Clement of Alexandria, and enabled him to turn back to the original sources of the Egyptian grammar and vocabulary. The whole range of science offers few other examples of a system built up from the base so completely, so unhesitatingly, and bearing upon it the stamp of truth and genius.

France realised the importance of the discovery and began the purchase of important archæological collections[1] as a basis for a department of Egyptian Antiquities in the Louvre. Champollion was appointed Keeper (1826), and he wrote a brief catalogue, a masterpiece of erudition for a science in its infancy. France thus endowed Egyptology with a museum which could be used as a practical laboratory. There still remained the work of resuming direct relations with Egypt that had been broken by the failure of Bona-

---

[1] *Report* to the Duke of Doudeauville upon the Egyptian collection purchased by order of H. M. at Livourne by M. Champollion, Junior (1826). The King of Sardinia had already organised a remarkable Egyptian Museum in Turin by the purchase of Drovetti's collection, which Champollion visited in Italy in order to test and improve his system of deciphering by the aid of the monuments themselves (*Lettres à M. le Duc de Blacas,* 1824 and 1826).

parte's expedition.   Champollion went to Egypt, explored the banks of the Nile, visited all accessible monuments, drew up a prodigious quantity of plans, and copied innumerable inscriptions during the months from August, 1828, to March, 1830. On his return, he was elected a member of the Académie des Inscriptions, and a professorship was founded for him at the Collége de France. But he delivered only a few lectures.   Exhausted by his labours, he died on March 12, 1831, leaving "as his visiting-card to posterity," to quote his own words, his *Grammar* and *Egyptian Dictionary* and the *Notes* written during his travels.[1]

It was by a miracle alone that Egyptology, after the death of its founder, escaped being wrecked by the heinous detraction of the classical scholars.   For fifteen years, its only opportunity for development was through the efforts of a few Orientalists, who, converted to the views of the master, tried to carry on his work: in France, Nestor Lhôte, Charles Lenormant, J. J. Ampére; in Italy, Rosellini and Ungarelli; in Holland, Leemans; in England, Wilkinson, Hincks, and Birch; in Germany, Lepsius.   The greatest of

[1] The publication of *Les Monuments de l'Égypte et de la Nubie* in two series, 4 vols. in folio of plates, and 2 vols. of *Notes* begun in 1835.

these was Lepsius, who led a memorable expedition to Egypt. The researches of Birch enlarged greatly the known vocabulary. At last, in 1846, came the man, whom all Egyptologists should, without national prejudice, regard as the veritable successor of Champollion—the Viscount Emmanuel de Rougé.

Under him Egyptology was again carried on with scientific discipline. In a letter to one of his disciples, François Chabas,[1] who, later, made for himself a name great in Egyptology, De Rougé thus defined the work that confronted them: "The completion of the *Grammar* and the *Dictionary* by a more rigorous method of investigation. In order to ascertain the meaning of a word, you must make this word explain itself in every passage in which it is found." This "long and arduous" test enabled De Rougé to publish critical editions of texts in which each word was discussed and studied so exhaustively that seven lines of an inscription required two hundred pages of explanation. But, by means of this method, the meaning of the words was established with such certainty that, even to-day, we find few details to correct in the texts translated by De Rougé.

[1] Upon De Rougé, Mariette, and Chabas, see *Notices biographiques* (*Bibliothèque égyptologique*, t. ix, xviii, xxi).

The new master had not yet seen Egypt, and he felt that the explorations that had proved so fruitful to his predecessors should be resumed. Meanwhile, another Frenchman, Auguste Mariette, had made for himself a name in Egypt by the discovery, near Memphis, south-west of Cairo, of the Serapeum, the monuments of which went to enrich the Louvre. He had interested the Khedive in the protection and the maintaining of the monuments and had been appointed Director of Archæological Works. He also founded a Museum at Boulak, which, to-day, is housed in Cairo. It was high time for intervention; the archæological campaigns of European scholars, and the traffic of the dealers in antiquities threatened to become more injurious to the monuments than the ravages of centuries. Mariette was entering upon a more methodical system of excavation and was already engaged in the publication of the more important documents when De Rougé arrived in Egypt. Can we realise the enthusiasm of the great scholar, prepared for his exploration by years of arduous labour in the privacy of his study, to whom the Egyptian tongue had revealed all its secrets, when he came face to face with the monuments and read the history recorded on their stones? De Rougé and his companions spent five months copying, photographing, collecting inscriptions, Mariette accompanying them everywhere, "placing himself, his skilled men, and his time at their disposal." It was only when he was overcome by illness, consequent upon his labours, that De Rougé returned to France.

No more than Champollion did his span of life permit him to co-ordinate for posterity all the intuitions and certitudes gained during his journey in Egypt. Nevertheless, his work was accomplished. His methodical researches, his vigorous translations revealed to the scientific world the vast scope and consequence of Champollion's discovery and compelled it to abandon its sceptical attitude. In France and elsewhere, it had been contended that hieroglyphics would never supply other material than royal names, dates, funeral formulæ, and prayers to the gods, and that the language was unfitted for literary or poetical purposes.

But the works of De Rougé and his contemporaries—Chabas, Devéria, De Horrack, in France; Heinrich Brugsch and J. Dümichen in Germany; Lepage-Renouf and Goodwin in England demonstrated step by step what an immense field of knowledge the deciphering of hieroglyphics had opened up to mankind.

It is not my purpose to quote the names of the Egyptian scholars of our own day, but I may briefly sum up the results thus far obtained.

In the domain of philology, Egyptian has proved to be a language related to the Semitic stock, but bearing African grafts, and its unbroken course can be traced—an almost solitary example—for over forty centuries, from the rudimentary morphology of primitive times down to the Coptic, alive beneath its mask of Greek.

In the domain of epigraphy, it has caused the problem of the origin of writing to come again under discussion.  Whence and how did writing originate?  What were the stages of its evolution?  Did man start with "ideographs"—picture-writing—and deform the pictorial signs till they deteriorated into conventional letters?  At what stage of development, and under what form did the Phœnicians borrow from Egypt an alphabet so serviceable that it is still, with very slight modifications, in use among the white races to-day?

But the domain most enriched by the discoveries of Egyptology is that of history, where the horizon suddenly receded four or five thousand years beyond the Homeric Age.  Above all its other qualifications, Egypt possesses that of providing an uninterrupted series of documents from the Neolithic times to those of the Græco-Roman civilisation. We observe in her history the beginnings of tribal life; of family life focussed in the tombs of its ancestors; the process of centralisation and the hegemony of one chief—the Pharaoh. We further see how Pharaoh, in his cumulative capacity of son of the gods, patron of the family cult, high-priest of the temple, mediator between gods and men, was able to consolidate his rule; how this concentration of power in one hand brought about a royal absolutism, out of which grew in later times the theory of an omnipotent, providential State in which the sovereign is the master, protector, and father of his subjects: how this ideal was further developed in the Roman Empire and found its last expression in modern Cæsarism.

In addition to history properly so-called, Egypt supplies information upon public and civil law, land tenure, and rights of property from archaic times, in documents which are not only numerous and legible, but of convincing reliability, owing to the designs and pictures with which they are illustrated. Of the life led by the prehistoric Egyptians during the Vth, XIIth, and XVIIIth dynasties, 3000, 2000, and 1500 years before Christ, we learn more every day, the garments they wore, the avocations they followed, their pleasures, their sorrows,—we know them all; we can form of them, not only an idea but a picture, more minute, accurate, and vivid in its details, than if we should endeavour to visualise to ourselves the same conditions in England or France in the time of Charlemagne, or even in a more recent period. The old rulers of Egypt we know better than our own kings; we know them in spirit and body, through their mummies and monuments which have been brought into the light of day. We are under the spell of a vast reach of civilisation revealed by tangible testimonies; here history is not established by abstract statements and scanty memorials; the documents conjure up the vision of the events themselves. The facts are actualised for us in their native atmosphere; the dead have come to life again upon the walls of their tombs, amidst the accustomed surroundings of their earthly homes, and they tell their own story to us, themselves.

Furthermore, Egyptian history is so intermingled with that of other nations, Syrians, Israelites, Assyrians, Persians, Greeks, that any new hieroglyphic text brought to light may be expected to supply fresh information on the history of the East. For instance, from one inscription, we read of the treaty of peace concluded between Ramses II and the princes of Asia Minor; from another, of the presence of the tribes of Israel in Syria; from another, of the campaigns of Ramses III against the "peoples of the sea," among whom are named the ancestors of the Sardinians, Achæans, and Sicilians. Although the documents are still silent upon the journeyings of the Israelites in Egypt and upon the influence of the Egyptian civilisation upon the Mosaic literature—a subject which arouses such passionate inquiry—they have thrown an unexpected light upon the life and customs of Syria in the fifteenth century B.C. as is seen in the diplomatic correspondence of the Pharaohs discovered at El-Amarna. And if we come to the Græco-Roman period of Egyptian civilisation, what precious treasures have recently come to light in the Greek papyri, written in Egypt: fragments of Greek tragedies, comedies of Menander, legal deeds, thousands of pages of family archives, to which should be added magic texts, religious hymns, popular legends, private and official correspondence, treatises on medicine and mathematics—memorials of every kind, written in demotic or hieratic on papyri of an earlier period. Mommsen, therefore, considering these papyri as sources of history, no less valuable than records on stone, could rightly prophesy that after our century of epigraphy, "the twentieth century would be the century of papyrology."

A fresh incentive was also given to research in another field, that of religious history. Herodotus says the Egyptians were the most religious of men. No other people allows us to follow the evolution of religious feeling throughout a period of the length of four thousand years, and by means of such testimonies as pictures still extant in their temples, and rituals inscribed on their papyri. Not only does Egypt offer a most fruitful field for the examination of the origin of metaphysical beliefs, that she may lend her aid to their solution. She seems to verify the words of Fustel de Coulanges: "Death was the first mystery and it led men into the way of all the other mysteries." To elude definitive death; to continue this earthly life in another world; to force a way by the help of magic into the world beyond,—such appear to have been the aspirations of the primitive Egyptians. Next was evolved the conception of a God, who is a Saviour and Redeemer, Osiris, who, yielding himself up unto death, opened the way of Eternal Life to men and transformed Death into Victory. Finally, Osiris the Saviour develops into Osiris the Judge, who weighs the hearts of men and admits to immortality only those who, like him, were righteous. We know how these ideas reacted upon the Græco-Roman world and how they prepared the way for Christianity.

And lastly, in the domain of art, it should be remembered, how ancient Egypt by her monuments alone, apart from any understanding of her script, which, here, is superfluous, has influenced powerfully the other nations in antiquity. No other country possessed to the same degree a style so entirely original, for her style was the outcome of her religious feelings. Art was in Egypt something more than an æsthetic manifestation, a fanciful creation of the mind, or the expression of a heart moved by Beauty, and therefore varying with temperament, liable to external influences. In Egypt, the plan and dimensions of the monuments, the idealistic or realistic rendering of a statue or bas-relief, the decoration of an edifice, even the shape and the details of a jewel, were controlled by a religious belief, ordained by a superstition. If a jewel is primarily a fetish, a magic charm, a magic contrivance of safety, and only secondarily an ornament, an article of attire, much more is a temple, a statue, a decoration, any work of art, an act of faith, the expression of a religious belief, the observance of a rite. Thus, tracing back artistic inspiration to its primitive source, we see that it is owing to her primeval creed and the force of her religious sentiment that Egypt has been able, throughout so many centuries, to maintain her art original, intact, aloof from foreign influence

Such, in brief, is the civilisation whose title-deeds have been restored to the archives of mankind by the genius of Champollion.   Despite the efforts of the little group who followed in the footsteps of the master, Egypt is still an unexploited field. The landmarks set up by the first pioneers only serve to point out what an immense unknown tract extends before them.   If worked with adequate forces, this prodigious field of research would yield more bounteous harvest than was ever reaped on the banks of the Nile.   But the labourers in it are few.   *Vita brevis, ars longa.*   May the students of our coming generation hearken to our call!   May they come in numbers, and whole-heartedly devote themselves to a task which shall reward them a hundred-fold and give to them a joy exceeding their highest hopes, if, like the initiate to the worship of Isis, they draw near to the hidden truths with their "inmost soul."

# INDEX

## A

Abousir, 2

Abydos, temple, 9, 100

Achilles, Shield of, decorations of Egyptian origin, 230, 231, 241, 247, 249

Ackerblad, Swedish scholar, interpreter of hieroglyphics, 260

*Adventures of Sinouhit, The,* 200–202

*Æneid,* on judgment, 123, 130

Agricultural legends, 104–106

Ahmasi, Queen, wife of Thotmes I, 12, 28; union with Amon-Râ, 18–19; bas-relief of *accouchement* of, 20

Ahmes I, victories, 43

Alasia, country of, 211

Amélineau, 100

Amenemhait, overseer of the flocks, 60

Amenemhait I, 200, 204

Amenemheb, officer of Thotmes III, 205, 206

Amenmes, 12

Amenophis II, 206

Amenophis IV, religious revolution of, 41 ff.; divine origin, 42; appearance, 45; parentage, 46; character, 47; changes his name, 49; relation to Aton, 52; builds temples to Aton, 52, 54; relations with priesthood, 45, 53; Reformer of the Faith, 54; in favour with the people, 55; Khounaton's Hymn, 55–58; encourages

realistic art, 65; statue of, 66; death, 67; influence, 68

Ammouianashi, Prince of Tonou, 200

"Amon, gardens of," 8, 37

"Amon of the Ways," 212

Amon-Râ, 16, 24, 69; union with Queen Ahmasi, 18 ff.; priesthood of, 24, 35, 44, 45, 48, 50, 53; disestablishment of, 41 ff.; union with Queen Moutemouâ, 42; relations with Kings of Egypt, 43, 44; worship of, forbidden, 49, 51; name effaced on monuments, 49, 51, 60; hymns to, 61; influence on Theban artists, 65; worship of, restored, 67; statue of, 212

Ampère, J. J. 271

Animals representing gods, 69

Anna, on the situation in Egypt at the death of Thotmes III, 32

Anti-feminist party, in Egypt, 16

Antiquities, in the Louvre, 270

Anubis, 78, 162; chapels of, 4, 9, 30; wars, 77

Apuleius, 154; on festival of *Navigium Isidis,* 165

Art, Theban school, 65; Egyptian, 230–246, 280

Asia, travels of Egyptians in, 199 ff.

Ati, 36

Aton, worship of, substituted for worship of Amon, 41 ff.; how represented, 51; relation to Khounaton, 52, 64;

283

# Index

www.ingramcontent.com/pod-product-compliance
Lightning Source LLC
Chambersburg PA
CBHW040406110426
42812CB00011B/2467